THE
LITTLE
BOOK
OF
TYRONE

CATHAL COYLE

The
History
Press
Ireland

This book is dedicated to my mother, Olive

First published 2014
This edition published 2018

The History Press Ireland
50 City Quay
Dublin 2
Ireland
www.thehistorypress.ie

British Library Cataloguing in Publication Data.
A catalogue record for this book is available from the British Library.

ISBN 978 0 7509 8787 5

Typesetting and origination by The History Press

CONTENTS

ACKNOWLEDGEMENTS

I have so many people to thank for helping towards the research and writing of this book. First of all I thank my wife Louise and my children, Caoimhe (who provided many of the drawings in this book), Dáire (who helped with some of the research) and Ruairí (for his helpful chats) for their love and support. I also must thank Beth Amphlett from The History Press who was kind enough to offer me this project after my initial suggestion.

My extended family have also been helpful and a big thanks to anyone who helped or offered advice in any way, including the Keightley Family for permission to use the photograph of Beaghmore Stone Circles.

Thanks to Ms Caroline Marshall for her permission to publish extracts of the following poems of W.F. Marshall from *Livin' in Drumlister* at various parts of this book: 'Purple and Gold', 'Me an' Me Da' and 'The Fairy Hill'. Thanks to Polly Devlin and The O'Brien Press for their permission to publish an extract from *The Far Side of the Lough* in Chapter 4. Thanks to the Tyrone GAA County Board for their permission to use the official county crest in Chapter 7. Thanks to The Gallery Press for permission to use the poetry of John Montague in Chapters 4 and 8. Thanks to the Ulster History Circle for their permission to use the image of the W.F. Marshall plaque in Chapter 8.

Thanks to all of the following for their professional assistance: David Currie (Irish Football Association); Pat Grimes (Moortown); Marian Hilley (Omagh District Council); Christine Johnston (Migration Studies Library, Ulster American Folk Park); Willow Murray (Irish Rugby Football Union); Dominic McCaughey (Tyrone GAA); Christine McGowan (Hill of the O'Neill and Ranfurly House Arts and Visitor Centre); Mary McKeown and Séamus Mac Giolla Phádraig (Cookstown District Council); Anne O'Neill (An Post); David Wishart (Dungannon Rugby Club).

INTRODUCTION

County Tyrone is part of the historic province of Ulster, and many significant 'arrivals' and 'departures' has helped to define its history. From the exit of famous clans during the 'Flight of the Earls' episode to the recent influx of a vast array of nationalities from around the world, the county has developed into a shining example of twenty-first-century life in Ireland.

Indeed, Tyrone or *Tír Eoghain* – Eoghan's land – is a diverse place in terms of its people and its landscape. The bustling towns of Dungannon and Cookstown in the south and Omagh and Strabane further north can be juxtaposed with the slower pace and tranquillity of the Glenelly Valley and small hamlets that are dotted around the county. It is a fine example of how the Planter and the Gael has co-existed since the times of the Plantation – while in more recent times the 'newcomers' from other European regions (and often further afield) who have decided that Tyrone offers them the opportunities that other places cannot.

Perhaps the irony about this new demographic is that Tyrone has historically been a county of emigration – particularly to North America and Australasia as people sought better opportunities when times were economically difficult in their native land. This has been recognised by the building of the magnificent Ulster American Folk Park that is situated between Omagh and Newtownstewart, which pays homage to the Diaspora of Tyrone and other Irish counties.

For those fortunate enough to have stayed in the 'O'Neill County', as it is often termed, the castles, lakes, mountains and forests are among the most beautiful and enchanting in the whole of Ireland.

One such attraction is Favour Royal Forest in Augher. It contains St Patrick's Chair and Well, symbolising the patron saint's close connection to Tyrone. Indeed, St Patrick is a popular title of many churches, sporting organisations and schools throughout the county.

The natural beauty of Tyrone is enhanced by the warmth and friendliness of its people. While there have been difficult times due to economic reasons and during the 'Troubles' of the twentieth century, Tyrone people are proud, resilient and talented. These key attributes have often translated into success on the international stage, whether it be the remarkable achievements of General James Shields from Altmore near Galbally, who became a senator in the United States Congress; or Elizabeth Noble from Dungannon, who became known as Sister Nivedita, a highly influential educationalist in India.

The county town of Omagh is a central location in Tyrone for sporting and cultural events, while further west the towns of Castlederg, Dromore and Trillick have also been noted for their musical and literary contributions down the years. The literary aspect to Tyrone life has been renowned since the days of William Carleton in the nineteenth century, and his famous aptitude for writing about the people and places of Tyrone, Ulster and Ireland has been carried on by respected writers such as Benedict Kiely and Brian O'Nolan.

The esteemed talents of musicians such as Paul Brady and Philomena Begley have also been internationally recognised, with their fabulous longevity and success both at home and in many other countries a tribute to their Tyrone roots.

In sporting terms, Tyrone individuals have achieved wonderful accolades and trophies: world titles in snooker, major titles in golf, along with success in team sports such as rugby, soccer and Gaelic games where Tyrone teams have made their mark on the highest stage. The inaugural All-Ireland Senior Gaelic football success for Tyrone in 2003 was almost a century in the making, but it was celebrated raucously. The legacy of this victory shouldn't be underestimated, as it planted a seed that will inspire future generations.

Tyrone has had its own often unique or indeed peculiar superstitions; for example, it was considered unlucky to be the first house to show smoke on a May morning, with the cattle being milked and the byre swept clean before the fire was lit. One cure worth mentioning is for deafness; that is to anoint an ear with the oil of eels!

Tyrone may be rapidly changing in a demographic sense but the natural beauty hasn't changed despite the passing of millennia – Beaghmore Stone Circles being a fine example. This group of Neolithic stones is a strong symbol that the past in Tyrone is often inescapable – and that our shared heritage and culture in the O'Neill County is to be cherished and treasured. Hopefully this book will remind us all of that.

Stone Circles at Beaghmore
Connor Keightley – March, 1995

Far away I hear you calling,
Motherland! Still dear to me;
When the autumn leaves are falling
I'll be back across the sea,
Tramping through the mist that gathers
Down from Sperrin's summits lone
To the homestead of my fathers
On the uplands of Tyrone.

W.F. Marshall 'The Bard of Tyrone', *Purple and Gold*

1

A POTTED HISTORY OF TYRONE

County Tyrone covers an area that is geographically and historically part of the Irish province of Ulster.

Tyrone gets its name from the Irish *Tír Eoghain*, meaning 'Eoghan's land', after the ancient division of north-west Ireland between the two sons of *Niall Noígiallach*, or Niall of the Nine Hostages, Conall and Eoghan. Most of what is now Donegal became *Tír Conaill*, or 'Conall's land', while the remainder went to Eoghan during the fifth century AD, who founded the kingdom of Aileach, later known as *Tír Eoghain*.

Before it became known as an Irish county, this area of *Tír Eoghain* referred to the large territory where Eoghan's descendant Hugh O'Neill exerted his authority – an area which included a large swathe of the present counties of Tyrone and Derry. The O'Neills ruled for hundreds of years and the influence that this dynasty had can still be seen today in villages and towns across the county; their stronghold, Dungannon, has been one of the most strategically important sites throughout the history of Ireland.

The concept of the 'county' was created by the English administration as the major subdivision of an Irish province in the years following the Anglo-Norman invasion of Ireland, but it wasn't until the sixteenth century that Tyrone became officially regarded by the English Tudors as a county.

These are some important milestones that had an impact on Tyrone and its people:

c. 7000–4000 BC: Archaeologists can trace the first human inhabitants in the north of Ireland back to this period, in what is termed the Mesolithic or Middle Stone Age. These were thought to be the very first immigrants to Ireland – possibly reaching the western shores of Lough Neagh from the River Bann. Flint tools dredged out of the Blackwater river date from this period. It is thought that these people survived by hunting, fishing and the gathering of wild plant foods.

c. 4000 BC: People began to clear the landscape in order to grow crops, which resulted in a reduction of natural forest throughout the northern part of Ireland. This period of history is termed the Neolithic or New Stone Age. Archaeologists identified the remains of cereals and domestic animal bones that mark the introduction of agriculture into the landscape, and the first settled farming communities established with animals being domesticated for use.

Perhaps one of the most important legacies left by the Neolithic farmers was their megalithic tombs for their honoured dead, or large earthen constructions used primarily as burial places. The emphasis placed on these megaliths in archaeological studies is mainly due to the fact that they are the only things to have survived largely intact from the Neolithic era. The construction of megaliths did not commence with the first Neolithic settlers. Rather, their construction began several centuries after the first arrivals, around 3500 BC.

Thanks to the excavation of forty-five prehistoric sites around County Tyrone, the evidence suggests that the four main tomb types (court, portal, passage and wedge) were present at various locations around Tyrone – there are 130 of them in total. These tombs consist of a burial chamber surrounded by a large mound of stone, and are the most prominent Neolithic field monuments.

Another ritual monument of the Neolithic period is the henge, with its ditch inside an outer bank (unlike that of the rath, which is outside). A Tyrone example is Dún Ruadh, meaning Red Fort, situated about 4 miles north of An Creagán in Mid-Tyrone.

c. 2500–600 BC: With the dawn of the Bronze Age in Ireland, there was the gradual introduction of metal into the everyday experience of people. Tyrone can boast of three gold lunulae (moon-shaped neck ornaments of the early Bronze Age) which were found at Tullanafoile, Trillick and Cregganconroe.

The first metal workers, the 'Beaker folk' (who arrived in Ireland from 1800 BC during the Middle Bronze Age), built their characteristic graves, which sometimes contained the pottery drinking vessels from which they have been named. Their wedge-shaped graves had a burial gallery of large upright stones, roofed with lintels, the grave narrowing and becoming lower towards the rear; Loughmacrory being one example.

Existing tool types, such as stone axes and flint knives, were transformed into new forms made in copper and bronze. During the Bronze Age people settled the landscape in ever-increasing numbers and much of the previously avoided lowlands, with their heavier soils, became occupied.

Beaghmore is a ritual site in Tyrone associated with the Early Bronze Age. In an area where bog was cleared, seven stone circles, ten alignments of stones and more than twelve cairns were found.

c. **500 BC onwards:** The first 'Celtic' immigrants arrived in Ireland soon after 500 BC and archaeologists term the period from then until AD 400 as the Iron Age. Habitation sites became more easily identifiable – some of these were in *crannógs* (artificial islands in lakes) which continued in use until the later Middle Ages.

The Celts had a highly structured society, with kings at the head. Under the kings were: the nobles, the warrior class, the *aes dána* (craftsmen), the freemen, and, at the bottom, the slaves.

The Celts also worshipped their gods: Lugh was lord of the first fruits of harvest. Men and women met at Lughnasa sites to celebrate Lugh with games, dancing and feats of strength.

OGHAM

The written form of the Celtic language known as Ogham is the earliest form of the Irish language. This twenty-five-letter alphabet was supposedly inspired by Ogma, God of Eloquence. It is a script that consists of a series of notches and strokes to represent the different letters of the alphabet. Surviving inscriptions usually consist of personal or tribal names. It is usually carved along the edge(s) of a large upright stone, beginning at the base and running upwards to, and over, the top, if necessary. While the main concentration of Ogham-inscribed stones is in the province of Munster, there is an Ogham-inscribed pillar stone at Aghascrebagh, about 4 miles from An Creagán in Tyrone.

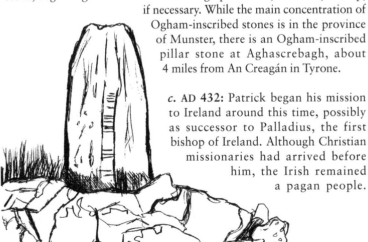

c. **AD 432:** Patrick began his mission to Ireland around this time, possibly as successor to Palladius, the first bishop of Ireland. Although Christian missionaries had arrived before him, the Irish remained a pagan people.

During the fifth century AD, Christianity was introduced to the north of Ireland on an increasingly wider scale.

The raths and *cashels* (ringforts) of our landscape were built from this time on until the 1000s. The Clogher ringfort was perhaps one of the first in the north of Ireland. The early Christians usually lived in circular raths enclosing huts and room for stock; for example the Gortalowry rath in Cookstown, which is inside the old Derryloran cemetery.

Saint Patrick concentrated much of his missionary efforts in the north of Ireland, and this included the founding of a monastery at Clogher. The churches at Ballyclog and Donaghmore are two other examples that are allegedly testament to St Patrick's influence. Ballyclog translates into English as 'the townland of the Bell' and recognises the association of the East Tyrone district with St Patrick's Bell.

Sixth to ninth centuries AD: The territorial expansion of the *Cenél nEógain* (descendants of Eoghan) from their Inishowen heartland brought them into contact with the Airgialla (a federation of various kingdoms) who controlled a large part of Ulster, including the present South and East Tyrone.

The middle part of the eighth century saw *Cenél nEógain* influence become secure within the area of County Tyrone, but the conflict between them lasted for three centuries – culminating in the Battle of Leth Cam in 827. This was a watershed in the history of Ulster as the victory of *Cenél nEógain* meant their dominance in the Mid-Ulster region for the next eight centuries.

Following the consolidation of *Cenél nEógain* within the former Airgialla region territories, the geo-political designation *Tír Eoghain* had, before the end of the tenth century, extended in meaning to cover what later became County Tyrone.

c. **eleventh century onwards:** Tyrone becomes the traditional stronghold of the various O'Neill clans and families, the strongest of the Gaelic Irish families in Ulster, surviving into the seventeenth century. Tullaghoge Fort came into historical prominence from this time when it was a dynastic centre and inauguration place of the *Cenél nEógain*.

1171: The Normans came to Ulster in small numbers; and whilst they built their bases near the sea coasts of Antrim and Down, they made occasional raids into Mid-Ulster, such as that on Errigal Keerogue in 1171.

1455: Henry, the son of Eoghan O'Neill, was ceremonially inaugurated as the 'Great O'Neill' at Tullaghoge.

1483: Henry resigns as chieftain; his eldest son Conn Mór is inaugurated.

1493: Conn Mór is murdered by his younger brother Henry Óg, and this leads to a prolonged civil war in *Tír Eoghain*.

1550s and '60s, Era of Shane O'Neill: Shane O'Neill was perhaps the most powerful man in Ulster during this era. Known to his own people as Seán an Díomas (Shane the Proud), Queen Elizabeth I recognised Shane as 'Captain' of Tyrone during his visit to London on 3 January 1562.

However, he went on to antagonise his Ulster neighbours, and in 1567, as the O'Neills crossed the River Swilly at Farsetmore, they met a furious onslaught of O'Donnells and MacSweeneys – and Shane was killed during the fighting that ensued.

1585: The chieftain Hugh O'Neill was granted the title of Earl of Tyrone by Elizabeth I on the understanding that he would accept English law (like most of the other Irish chieftains) and introduce English reform policy throughout Tyrone and Ulster.

1598, The Rebellion of Hugh O'Neill: Although Hugh O'Neill had worked closely with the English Crown, he eventually grew disillusioned by its draconian policies, especially those that threatened his land. He began plotting a revolt in the late 1580s, building a formidable army, making contact with Catholic Spain, and formed an alliance with other Ulster chieftains, most notably with Red Hugh O'Donnell. The Nine Years' War, as it was later known, began in 1594. The following year Hugh secured the title of 'The O'Neill' or chief of the O'Neill clan from Turlough Luineach O'Neill.

Hugh O'Neill led other Irish clans in their revolt against Queen Elizabeth. For some years they were successful, including in 1598 when O'Neill routed the English army at the Battle of Yellow Ford when Hugh O'Donnell and Hugh Maguire attacked Henry Bagenal's Crown forces on the march with his 4,000 men and wiped out half his army.

1601: Hugh O'Neill is defeated at the Battle of Kinsale on Christmas Eve; this signals the end of Gaelic Supremacy in Tyrone.

1603, The Flight of the Earls: Two years after O'Neill's defeat at Kinsale, following the death of Elizabeth I, Hugh O'Neill made peace with the new king, James I, and the Treaty of Mellifont was signed. This restored the earls of Ulster to substantial land holdings and family ties; however, they felt uneasy with the growing numbers of English settlers. Some began to plot a renewed rebellion, again involving Spanish assistance. However, their English enemies, resenting that the Irish lords had been allowed to keep their lands, and suspicious of their loyalty to the Crown, tried to reduce the Irish lords' power. Facing renewed restrictions from the English regime and fearful of being charged with treason, Hugh O'Neill and his supporters chose to flee.

On 4 September 1607, O'Neill and other northern earls boarded a French ship at Rathmullan in Donegal to sail for the continent. They eventually landed in the Spanish Netherlands and from there proceeded to Rome, where they lived out their years on modest papal pensions. O'Neill died there in 1616 at the age of 76.

Within months of the departure of Hugh O'Neill and his followers, their lands were confiscated by the Crown and the path was clear for the Ulster Plantation.

Early seventeenth century, Ulster Plantations: With 500,000 acres of land now in its possession, the English Crown began a settlement scheme known as the Ulster Plantation, which commenced in 1609. The Irish Lord Deputy, Sir Arthur Chichester, was convinced the only way to control Ulster was to plant it with English and Scottish settlers. If people couldn't prove their ownership of land, it was confiscated from them and given to the new settlers.

The scheme's main objectives were to increase popular loyalty to England by greatly increasing the non-Irish settlers, in essence 'urbanising' parts of Ulster and improving the economy of Ireland and therefore increasing the Crown revenues. It provided opportunities for landless nobles from England and Scotland.

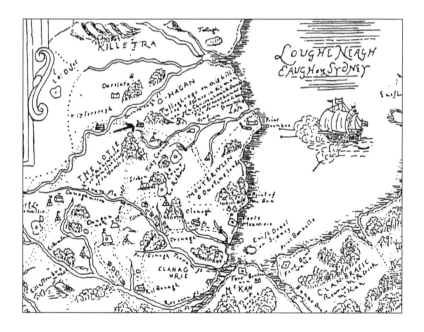

Tyrone was divided into five 'precincts':

Omagh, 11,000 acres
Strabane, 13,500 acres
Clogher, 12,500 acres
Mountjoy, 9,500 acres
Dungannon, 16,000 acres

1614: The Royal Charter to establish a free school in County Tyrone was laid down by King James I in 1608, resulting in the Royal School Dungannon being established by 1614, originally at Mountjoy near Lough Neagh.

1641: The resentment of those who had lost their lands in the Ulster Plantation or who now paid high rents for their land came to the surface. They were determined to win back their lands from the new settlers. An uprising was planned for 23 October 1641 but on the night before this, government officials in Dublin received information about the plot and arrested some of the main protagonists. However, the rebellion or rising (depending on one's perspective) went ahead as planned, and thousands of Protestant settlers were killed.

1646: The Scots army of General Robert Monro had arrived in Ulster in 1642 to aid the settlers, but four years later he received a crushing defeat at the hands of Owen Roe O'Neill's army at the Battle of Benburb. Owen Roe was the nephew of Hugh O'Neill.

1649: This 'rising' led to a trenchant response, especially with the arrival of Oliver Cromwell in Ireland, and led to the introduction of the Penal Laws against Roman Catholics across Ireland. Tyrone, as the chief centre of the rising, suffered most. Every surviving Catholic landowner of Irish stock lost his property as well as most of the lesser tenants.

THE PENAL LAWS

These were a series of laws that were also used against Protestant non-conformists, such as Presbyterians. Some of these included:

Exclusion from the legal professions and the judiciary
Exclusion from most public offices (Catholics since 1607, Presbyterians since 1707)

All alike had to pay 'tithes' (taxes – usually a tenth of income) for the support of the Church of Ireland. There were also commercial and trade restrictions which applied to the whole population: embargoes were placed on the export of wool, cattle and later, glass.

1724: The linen trade was flourishing throughout parts of Tyrone and free wheels and spindles were distributed to qualified persons throughout the county. It was the O'Neills who had originally fostered the making of linen, and until the seventeenth century it was for home use only.

Weaving predominated to the east of the county, spinning to the west. The popularity of linen meant that weaving occupied at least half of the male population (some full-time and the rest during slack times in the farming year) and most farmhouses had a loom which was constantly in use during the winter months.

Markets such as the one in Dungannon traded in flax, yarn and linen, both bleached and brown, although after 1728 it was only brown linen that was sold in the markets.

ESTABLISHMENT OF THE FOUR MAIN TOWNS IN TYRONE

Cookstown: The original town was built in about 1609, but was destroyed in the rebellion of 1641. The present town was built about 1750.

Dungannon: In 1609, it became a planned municipality with its Market Square, Scotch Street and Irish Street. It was awarded a charter in 1612.

Omagh: Omagh began to develop a reputation as a fortress town by the middle of the fifteenth century when the occupant of the castle was Art O'Neill. Most of the town of Omagh was destroyed by fire in 1742, but it recovered and by 1768 Omagh had replaced Dungannon as the county town of County Tyrone.

Strabane: James Hamilton, the Earl of Abercorn, came to Strabane as the Jacobean grantee, and his castle was built in 1609. The earl proceeded to build the town, which became a borough in 1612.

1771: One of Tyrone's most famous industries, Tyrone Crystal, was founded in Dungannon by Benjamin Edwards. It also had the distinction of being the first Irish crystal producer.

1782–93, Dungannon Convention Meetings: On 15 February 1782, delegates from 147 Volunteer Corps (these were local militias in the late eighteenth century that were raised to defend Ireland from the threat of French and Spanish invasion) met at the Presbyterian church in Dungannon.

During the first meeting (there were a total of four meetings) the delegates pledged support for resolutions advocating legislative independence for Ireland, whilst proclaiming their loyalty to the British Crown.

This marked the beginning of a politically active era in Ireland, and was an attempt by Roman Catholics and Presbyterians to seek relief from the Penal laws and trade restrictions.

1795–98: The Orange Order was formed in Loughgall in the neighbouring county of Armagh during 1795. This Protestant organisation soon became well organised throughout Tyrone, while on the Catholic side there were similar groups such as the 'Ribbonmen'.

The revolutionary United Irishmen's strength was seen in the members in Tyrone increasing from 4,855 in October 1796 to around 14,000 by May 1797, but no serious fighting occurred in Tyrone during the 1798 rising, unlike parts of Antrim and Down.

1800–01, The Act of Union: Following the United Irishmen's failed rising in 1798, the British Government, under Prime Minister William Pitt, decided to unify the Dublin and Westminster parliaments. This meant that Irish political representation transferred to Westminster. The United Kingdom of Great Britain and Ireland came into existence on 1 January 1801.

Tyrone returned two MPs to represent the county in the British Parliament at Westminster. As Catholics were excluded from qualifying as voters until 1793 and taking seats in Parliament until 1829, it wasn't until the electoral reforms which took effect in 1885 that most adult males became voters.

In these circumstances most Members of Parliament came from a limited number of aristocratic and gentry families, and there were few contested elections. The first two MPs who represented Tyrone at Westminster were James Stewart and Viscount Corry, both co-opted on 1 January 1801.

1802: *A Statistical Survey* was published by John McEvoy; this was a valuable account of the state of agriculture, political economy, labour wages and conditions in County Tyrone at the beginning of the nineteenth century.

1804: Whilst the Dublin–Belfast mail route had opened about a decade before, there was a coach connection established between Dungannon and Newry during this year, and another ran from Aughnacloy–Caledon–Dungannon.

1815: A coach connection was established between Dungannon and Armagh.

1829: The passing of the Roman Catholic Relief Act in Ireland led to the gradual erosion of the Penal Laws, giving Catholics full civil and political rights.

1838: On 31 July, an Act 'for the more effectual Relief of the Destitute Poor in Ireland' was passed. Unions were to be formed based on electoral divisions, which in turn were composed of townlands.

1839: Poor Law Unions were initiated in the four largest towns in Tyrone: Cookstown, Dungannon, Omagh and Strabane. Omagh was formally declared on 9 May and covered an area of 272 square miles. Its operation was overseen by an elected Board of Guardians, representing its twenty-nine electoral divisions; Dungannon Poor Law Union was formally declared just a few months later – on 20 July – and covered an area of 160 square miles. The site later became the home of the South Tyrone hospital.

1841: The new Omagh Union workhouse was erected on a 6-acre site to the north of Omagh. Designed by the Poor Law Commissioners' architect George Wilkinson, the building was based on one of his standard plans to accommodate 800 inmates.

The workhouse was declared fit for the reception of 'paupers' on 24 August 1841 and admitted its first inmates on the same day. Discipline in the workhouse was strict. Some of the offences and their punishments recorded in the Strabane workhouse during the 1840s included:

Refusing work – twelve stripes of a rod
Stealing money – fourteen stripes and eight cold baths over four weeks
Throwing stones and annoying a lunatic – twenty stripes, or twelve hours confinement, loss of a meal, and cold shower
Running away from workhouse – no milk for fourteen days
Stealing food – no milk for two days

1845–49: The Great Famine (*An Gorta Mór*) in County Tyrone. Statistical records indicate that Tyrone was among the counties least affected by famine. However, an estimated 11,500 people in Tyrone were sustained by public works (a government relief scheme) from mid-November 1846 until the end of March 1847.

The worst affected areas (statistically) were Omagh and Clogher Poor Law Unions, each of which had nearly 21 per cent of its population in receipt of food, and elsewhere in the county some local communities were affected by suffering owing to the famine. Some examples included:

Urney parish in early November 1846: 'The people are almost in despair at no work having commenced ...'

Strabane: 'Destitution in this town and neighbourhood is very great ... we have 340 families on our list to be relieved.'

Clonoe: 'The distress ... is beyond all description ... the majority are now in a state of the greatest destitution and many of absolute starvation.'

1869: The Irish Church Act disestablishes the Church of Ireland. It repeals the law that requires tithes to be paid to it. The act came into force on 1 January 1871.

1876: The top ten landowners in Tyrone owned 242,277 acres, which represented nearly one third of the total acreage in the county.

1879: The Great Northern Railway connects Dungannon with Cookstown.

1881: The census reveals the denominational breakdown of the population in Tyrone:

Total population: 197,719
Catholic: 109,793
Anglican: 44,256
Presbyterian: 38,564
Others: 5,106

1885: In the Parliamentary Reform Redistribution Act that took effect that year, County Tyrone was divided into four single-member constituencies: East Tyrone, Mid-Tyrone, North Tyrone and South Tyrone. The Franchise Act dramatically increased the number of voters, giving many Catholics and labourers of all denominations the right to vote for the first time.

This was a watershed election, probably the first where Catholics and Protestants divided voting into different 'blocs'. Three of the four constituencies voted Nationalist candidates; North Tyrone saw the Conservative candidate Lord Hamilton elected.

South Tyrone: William O'Brien (Nationalist)
North Tyrone: Lord Ernest Hamilton (Conservative)
Mid-Tyrone: Matthew Kenny (Nationalist)
East Tyrone: W. J. Reynolds (Nationalist)

HOME RULE: THE GROWTH OF UNIONISM AND NATIONALISM

During the late nineteenth century in Tyrone, as in the rest of the province of Ulster, the two 'traditions' began to organise more coherently into two factions along sectarian lines: Catholics became increasingly Nationalist in their outlook (i.e. they favoured a Home Rule Parliament in Dublin and separation from Britain); while Protestants (the vast majority who were already Unionist-minded especially after the Act of Union in 1801) were totally against the concept of Home Rule for Ireland. Apart from interfering with the industrial strength of Ulster counties, Home Rule was perceived to have the potential to give the Roman Catholic Church a greater say in the running of Government (this notion later translated into the unionist phrase: 'Home Rule is Rome Rule'). This convinced unionists that their religious and civil liberties would be threatened and also the entire concept of 'independence' could destabilise the union between Britain and Ireland.

1886: The First Home Rule Bill defeated in Westminster.

1893: The Second Home Rule Bill defeated in Westminster.

1901: The United Irish League (which supported Home Rule) was introduced into Tyrone with the establishment of branches in the middle and east of the county.

1904: The Tyrone County Board of the GAA was founded on Sunday 31 January in St Patrick's Hall, Dungannon.

1912: Ulster's Solemn League and Covenant. On Saturday 28 September, thousands of Unionists from throughout County Tyrone and the rest of Ulster signed the covenant that opposed Home Rule and demanded that the union between Ireland and Britain be maintained on 'Ulster Day'.

Only men could sign the Covenant. There was another version of it for their wives, mothers and sisters to sign; interestingly, of the 471, 414 signatures collected on Ulster Day, more came from the women than from men.

1914: The third Home Rule Bill was passed at Westminster on 25 May and placed on the Statute Book; however, the bill was subsequently suspended until the conclusion of the First World War.

1916: The Easter Rising in Dublin. Thomas Clarke from Dungannon was one of the leaders and the first signatory of the Proclamation of the Irish Republic. He was executed on 3 May in Kilmainham Jail.

1918: The General Election in December across Ireland returned three MPs in Tyrone. The county had a Nationalist majority of 5,149 (30,142 Nationalist to 24,993 Unionist votes) and it was now divided into three constituencies:

North-East Tyrone: Thomas Harbison, Irish Parliamentary Party
North-West Tyrone: Arthur Griffith, Sinn Fein
South Tyrone: William Coote, Unionist

TYRONE AND PARTITION

On 23 December 1920, the Government of Ireland Act entered the Statute Book, politically dividing Ireland. County Tyrone became part of the newly created political jurisdiction of Northern Ireland. Unionists were delighted with this outcome, despite the loss of three other Ulster counties from the new arrangement. However, there was a hope on the part of many Nationalists within the county that Tyrone might be excluded, given that a proposed 'Boundary Commission' (included in the signing of the Anglo-Irish Treaty of 6 December 1921) would include most, if not all, of Tyrone within the Irish Free State.

In administrative terms, partition meant that the Tyrone County Council was based in the county town of Omagh, while the Government of Northern Ireland was based at Stormont Estate near Belfast.

GERRYMANDERING

Many Nationalist-controlled local authorities pledged their allegiance to Dáil Éireann. However, the Stormont Home-Affairs Minister Dawson Bates dictated the positioning of electoral boundaries to favour Unionist candidates in elections.

This strategy was known as 'Gerrymandering' and was especially prevalent in counties such as Tyrone, Derry and Fermanagh. In Omagh Rural Council, for example, Nationalists cast 5,381 more votes than Unionists, but the new electoral boundaries gave Unionists in that area a majority of eighteen.

THE BOUNDARY COMMISSION

In December 1924, three members of the Boundary Commission and their staff visited Tyrone as part of an informal tour of the borderline. However, the collapse of the Boundary Commission during the final few months of 1925 dashed Nationalist hopes for inclusion into the Free

State; while Unionists living in border areas who had feared that their land would be handed over to the Free State were satisfied. The proposals of the Boundary Commission were considered so insignificant that the existing border which ran along county lines was retained.

1930s: The 'Depression' years of this decade were felt across the world and were triggered by the Wall Street Crash of 1929. This led to high levels of unemployment and emigration from Tyrone and other parts of Ireland, as it did again seventy years later.

1941: On 9 December, the building of an airbase commenced in the townland of Kinrush in Ardboe. Initially the airfield was occupied by the Royal Air Force, but was quickly given over to the USAAF (United States Army Air Forces). The airfield (known as Cluntoe) was used as a training base, and by 1943 over 3,500 American troops were stationed there.

1947: The Education (Northern Ireland) Act leads to the possibility of secondary and university education for many people from less advantaged backgrounds in Tyrone. The age of transfer between primary and secondary schools was set at 11, when it was believed that the average child had mastered the skills of reading, writing and arithmetic and was ready to learn new subjects.

1967: The Northern Ireland Civil Rights Association (NICRA) was established in January. It had an influential Tyrone input as Dr Con McCluskey from Dungannon was its first vice-chairman. Their initial impact was in organising protest marches and some of their basic aims included:

One man/one vote in council elections
Ending of 'gerrymandered' electoral boundaries
Fair allocation of public housing

1968: On 20 June the first protest in the 1968 Civil Rights campaign occurred in the village of Caledon. On 24 August the first Civil Rights March (organised by NICRA) took place from Coalisland to Dungannon.
   A new Tyrone Crystal company was founded during 1968 when Father Austin Eustace set up a factory to provide employment for the young people of the East Tyrone area. It enjoyed over forty years' successful trading until closing in March 2010.

1969: The beginning of the 'Troubles' period in Northern Ireland. Bernadette Devlin from Cookstown won a seat in the Westminster Parliament. She was the youngest woman to be elected to the House of Commons at Westminster.

1973: Under the organisational reforms carried out in Northern Ireland during this year, the county ceased to exist as a single administrative unit and was divided into various smaller units, which included the formation of district councils and Education and Library Boards. The first elections to the new district councils – the first voting by Proportional Representation (PR) in Northern Ireland since 1925 – took place on 30 May.

1985: Dennis Taylor from Coalisland won the World Snooker Title, defeating Steve Davis in the final at the Crucible Theatre in Sheffield.

1988: Windmill Primary School in Dungannon became the first 'Integrated' (i.e. inclusive of Catholic and Protestant) school in Tyrone.

1998: 15 August: one of the darkest days in Tyrone's history. Thirty-one people died (twenty-eight people died on the day, as well as two unborn children and an injured man died three weeks later) as a result of an explosion in Omagh town centre. There were also hundreds of people injured. The bomb had been planted by the 'real' Irish Republican Army.

2001: Dungannon Rugby Club won the All-Ireland League Division One Title, defeating Cork Constitution at Lansdowne Road.

2003: On 28 September, Tyrone won their first All-Ireland Senior Football Championship when they defeated Armagh by 0–12 to 0–9 at Croke Park, Dublin.

2011: Darren Clarke from Dungannon won golf's Open Championship at Royal St George's in Kent, England by three shots – the first golf 'major' title for a Tyrone person.

The 2011 Northern Ireland Census reveals that County Tyrone had a population of approximately 177,986.

2014: First elections to the new local 'super councils' – Tyrone areas are included in three new council areas. These are Mid-Ulster, Fermanagh and Omagh, Derry and Strabane.

2016: The three County Tyrone-based constituencies all voted in favour of remaining within the European Union in the Referendum Vote held on 23rd June.

2017: Tyrone retain the Ulster Senior Football Championship after defeating Down by 2-17 to 0-15 at Clones.

2

'AMONG THE BUSHES': CASTLES, FORESTS AND HIGH CROSSES

County Tyrone possesses a wonderful array of natural and man-made features and visitor attractions. The county shares the Sperrin Mountains with neighbouring County Derry along much of its eastern border, whilst in South Tyrone the hilly range, which includes Slieve Beagh and the 'drumlin' area of the Clogher Valley, is situated on the Fermanagh and Monaghan borders.

The western region of the county is marked by the River Derg flowing eastwards to the Foyle catchment. To the east lies Lough Neagh, the largest body of freshwater in Ireland and the Ballinderry river flows through the eastern uplands, draining into Lough Neagh to the east of Cookstown.

Tyrone has a wealth of prehistoric and early Christian period monuments as well as the castles, forests and other visitor attractions that are dotted around the county. In the past century, the National Trust has included a few cultural attractions under its remit, including Wellbrook Beetling Mill near Cookstown.

'AMONG THE BUSHES'

County Tyrone earned the phrase 'Among the Bushes' after the Strabane-born poet William Collins (see Chapter 8) referred to his native county in the poem 'A Sigh for Old Times':

O God be with the good old times when I was twenty-one
In Tyrone among the bushes, where the Finn and Mourne run
among the field and meadows, fair by Mourne winding way or the
slopes of Knockavoe,
bedecked heather brown that rises o'er the Mourne shore.

PREHISTORIC MONUMENTS

There are more than 1,500 megalithic (derived from two Greek words – *mega* and *lithos* – meaning great stone) tombs in Ireland, concentrated in the north and north-east of Ireland; and Tyrone has 130 of them.

The main recognised tomb types (namely court tombs, portal tombs, passage tombs and wedge tombs) are all found in County Tyrone. Among the prehistoric monuments in County Tyrone includes Beaghmore Stone Circles and Knockmany Passage Grave.

Beaghmore Stone Circles

Located 8.5 miles north-west of Cookstown, on the fringe of the Sperrin Mountains, Beaghmore is an impressive series of Bronze Age ceremonial stone monuments that was excavated from the surrounding bog between 1945 and 1949 and also in 1965. It was first excavated by the archaeologist A. Mc L. May in 1945, who revealed three pairs of stone circles, all under a metre in height, and one circle standing alone which is filled with over 800 stones. Archaeologists believe that these date back to around 1500 BC.

Beaghmore means 'Large Birch Wood' and seven stone circles and ten alignments of stones along with several cairns were revealed under the peat of this preserved site. The stone circles occur in pairs, with associated small cairns and stone alignments. 'The Dragon's Teeth' is a single large circle filled with closely set stones.

What these stones actually mean remains uncertain. The stones seem to have been positioned with some reference to the seasons, the sun or the moon but perhaps the circles, alignments and cairns had a ritual function for restoring fertility.

Cregganconroe Court Grave and Creggandevesky Court Tomb

Not that far apart, Cregganconroe is located on a small hill 3 miles north of Pomeroy, while Creggandevesky is 2.5 miles north of neighbouring Carrickmore.

Cregganconroe is an impressive tomb that has massive portal stones but few other stones of its shallow forecourt survive. It leads into a two-chambered gallery, past a large fallen lintel. Behind the gallery are two lateral chambers opening symmetrically into each of the long sides of the cairn, which is 27 yards long and includes large boulders. Though roofless, these subsidiary chambers resemble small portal tombs.

Its near neighbour Creggandevesky was a long mound with an oval forecourt – and was excavated between 1979 and 1982. It was found to be in an excellent state of preservation, with flint implements and Neolithic pottery discovered during this time. This tomb, which has an impressive entrance with massive lintel, is built at the head of a valley

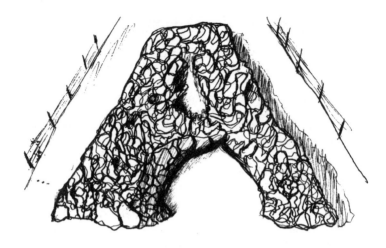

extending westward with excellent views (on a good day). Excavation showed that the back of the tomb was partially robbed in prehistoric times, and that it was built about 3500 BC.

Knockmany Passage Tomb

This passage tomb cemetery is located 2 miles from Augher and 3 miles from Clogher, and is reached by an uphill path through the forest from the nearby car park. Formerly known as 'Annia's Cove' it would originally have been approached through a passage, of which little remains. The position commands extensive views of the surrounding countryside in all directions. The covering cairn in its present form is modern, added in 1959 to protect the stones from weathering.

Excavation showed that a stone cairn capped with earth within a stone revetment originally covered the burial chamber. The passage of a 'classic' passage grave is absent but four of the upright stones of the chamber are decorated with characteristic passage-grave art, including circles, spirals and zigzags. Knockmany probably dates from the Neolithic era – around 3000–2500 BC.

Also located close to Augher is St Patrick's Chair and Well. This visitor attraction is also known as the 'Druid's Chair and Well' – located on the hillside in Altadaven Glen. This large sandstone monument appears to be the shape of a chair and is believed to have healing properties.

Loughmacrory Wedge Tomb

This fine wedge tomb is located near An Creagán in Mid-Tyrone. This burial chamber has a front chamber and a doorway marked by three stones, and is notable for the large thorn (fairy) tree growing from its middle. The Loughmacrory Wedge Tomb is believed to have been constructed around 2000 BC. Visitors to this feature can also enjoy viewing the flora and fauna of the Loughmacrory Lakeside Walk.

Sess Kilgreen Passage Tomb

When translated, Sess Kilgreen means 'the sixth part of a sunny wood'. This passage tomb is locally known as 'the Fort' and is located off the main Ballygawley to Omagh road. Like Knockmany, this tomb is roofless and has no passage. Sess Kilgreen is probably the best ornamented tomb known in Ulster, with its worn decoration clearly visible on two of its stones, in the form of concentric circles similar to others in the Boyne Valley in the province of Leinster.

EARLY CHRISTIAN PERIOD MONUMENTS

There are a number of important monuments from this period in County Tyrone – including the high crosses at Ardboe and Donaghmore in the east of the county.

Ardboe Cross

Ardboe Cross is located in the townland of Farsnagh, close to the mid-point of the western shore of Lough Neagh; it marks the area of a monastery associated with St Colman, thought to be founded in the sixteenth century.

The monastery was burned in 1166, destroying any early wooden structures, but a medieval parish church was later built on the site. This sandstone cross is believed to be the first high cross of Ulster, standing at 18.5ft high and 3.5ft wide, with twenty-two panels with a scheme of biblical carving.

On the east (Old Testament) face the carvings include Adam and Eve, the sacrifice of Isaac, and Christ in glory with scales and flames beneath. The west (New Testament) side has the visit of the magi and the wedding feast at Cana, while on the south side of the cross are Cain and Abel, and David killing Goliath. The scenes on the north side appear to represent the early life of Christ including his baptism.

A tenth-century date has been suggested for the erection of Ardboe Cross. There is also the ruins of St Colman's Abbey and a church (believed to have been built in the sixteenth century) in the graveyard.

Donaghmore Cross

Donaghmore Cross is at a road junction at the west end of Donaghmore's main street, outside the old graveyard. This 6-yard tall sandstone cross dates from the ninth century and has survived from an early monastery on or near its present site, traditionally said to have been founded by St Patrick.

The present cross is made up of parts of two separate crosses, the base and lower shaft not quite the same as the upper shaft and head. Its decoration includes an interesting mixture of figure carving and motifs in distinctive circular, diamond-shaped and semicircular frames.

On the east side are the annunciation to the shepherds, the adoration of the magi, the wedding feast at Cana, the miracle of loaves and fishes, the arrest and the crucifixion. On the west side are Adam and Eve, Cain and Abel and the sacrifice of Isaac. There is a solitary horseman, perhaps unfinished, on the west side of the base.

Errigal Keerogue Cross

Errigal Keerogue Cross and church is located in Gort townland, 3 miles west of Ballygawley. It is believed to have been founded by St MacCairthenn, who died in 506. This ridge-top graveyard overlooks the Clogher Valley, and the stone cross has the features of a Celtic cross inscribed on it. An early monastery associated with St Ciaran (Dachiarog) and the medieval parish church (said to date from 1489) was based at this site: St Ciaran's Well is situated nearby. According to legend, the Normans invaded the area in 1171.

Aghascrebagh 'Ogham' Stone

This is one of the very few Ogham stones in the north of Ireland (the main concentration of these stones is in Munster). Situated 4 miles north of An Creagán, it is only a yard high. The stone had fallen and has been re-erected on its little mound of stones.

The marks on the edges of this stone are characters from the Ogham alphabet that was used in fifth-century Ireland. The much-worn inscription has been interpreted as *DOTETTO MAQI MAGLANI* (Dotetto son of Maglani) – of which only seven letters can now be read. Behind it can be seen the much taller standing-stone.

Tullaghoge Fort

Tullaghoge Fort is located in Ballymully Glebe townland, on the main Stewartstown to Cookstown road. This magnificent rounded hilltop enclosure commands wide views and, planted with trees, is visible from miles around. It is a site of huge historical and cultural significance, and attracts hundreds of visitors each year.

The site came into historical prominence from the eleventh century when it was a dynastic centre and inauguration place of the *Cenél nEóghain*. The inauguration ceremony was conducted by the throwing of a shoe over the head of the new O'Neill, to indicate that he would follow in the footsteps of his distinguished ancestors who had borne the title.

The ceremony took place on a large stone chair thought to have been blessed by St Patrick, which stood on a hillside nearby; but this was destroyed in 1602 by Lord Mountjoy, in accordance with the Elizabethan policy of destroying all Irish symbols of clan allegiance. This marked the end of sacral kingship in Ireland and the end of the O'Neills, with Hugh O'Neill's inauguration in 1595 being the last to take place at Tullaghoge Fort.

The area has been redeveloped and signs directing visitors towards the site have been installed in Cookstown district. It remains a popular tourist destination during the summer months, and in 1998 a Spanish descendant of Hugh O'Neill – Don Carlos O'Neill – held an event to commemorate the inauguration ceremony of the O'Neills on the exact spot where the O'Neills were crowned the High Kings of Ulster in centuries gone by.

MEDIEVAL MONUMENTS

During this period in Tyrone's history, many castles and churches were constructed. Some examples include:

Harry Avery's Castle

Located in the village of Newtownstewart, the ruins of this castle named after Henry Aimbreidh O'Neill (who died in 1392) dates from the late fourteenth or early fifteenth century, and was possibly built by him. It is a stone castle deep in Gaelic Ulster, with a tower that looks like a gatehouse, entered between high D-shaped towers. The castle is especially important in relation to the study of native Irish medieval life prior to the plantation period.

Cappagh Old Church and Graveyard

The main body of this church dates back to the sixteenth century, but this site may have been used as a church site since the Early Christian Period. A bell associated with this parish, known as the Cappagh Bell, is in the National Museum of Ireland in Dublin.

Mountjoy Castle

Named after Elizabeth I's Viceroy Lord Mountjoy, this castle is thought to have succeeded an earlier O'Neill fortification. It is located 3 miles from Stewartstown, and stands on a low hill overlooking Lough Neagh. It is a small early seventeenth-century (built around 1605) three-storey building in the shape of a rectangle, captured by Sir Phelim O'Neill's forces in 1641 and burnt the following year. However, it was restored by the English and the forts in this area continued in use until the late seventeenth century.

PLANTATION PERIOD AND LATER MONUMENTS

The era of the plantation brought different styles of castles and churches as well as the introduction of country estates favoured by the English and Scottish settlers. Some examples include:

Baronscourt Estate
Located near Newtownstewart in a sheltered valley, it has been the home of the Duke of Abercorn's family since 1612, combining great historical and architectural interest with a landscape of outstanding natural beauty. Today this is a vibrant working farm. The herd of Japanese sika deer were initially introduced into a deer park in 1751, but since 1920 they have existed wild on the estate.

Benburb Castle
Situated on the cliff edge above the River Blackwater and within the grounds of the current Servite monastery in Benburb, Shane O'Neill had built a castle on this site in the mid-1500s. By 1611 the area was in English hands and a castle and bawn was erected by Sir Richard Wingfield on or near the same site. Now known as Benburb Castle, the nineteenth-century house in the bawn is privately occupied.

Castle Caulfield
This castle inspired the name of the village in which it is based. Erected in 1611 by Sir Toby Caulfield (who became Lord Charlemont in 1620), it has an interesting collection of octagonal chimney stacks and is noted for its lack of fortification. However, its mullioned windows survived the burning of the castle in 1641. A number of famous visitors include St Oliver Plunkett (who held a service there in 1670), as well as the founder of Methodism, John Wesley, who preached here in 1767.

Davies Bawn
Built by Sir John Davies around 1612, the ruins consist of a rectangular bawn with the remains of a number of square flankers at each corner still visible. This was once a site of strategic importance on the River Derg. The bawn would have been a refuge for planter families in the Castlederg area and was eventually rendered unfit for occupation after an attack by Sir Phelim O'Neill. The damage was never repaired.

Derryloran Church

Situated on the outskirts of Cookstown beside the Ballinderry river, a monastery is thought to have been founded on this site by St Luran. A church here was plundered in 1195 and the medieval parish church was on this site was possibly rebuilt around 1620, and remained in use for the following two centuries, until 1822.

Newtownstewart Castle

The Planter's castles tended to be of the Elizabethan manor house style, as at Newtownstewart, although many (like this one) were burnt down in the rebellion of 1641 in Ulster. Also known as Stewart Castle, this building effectively closes the vista at the foot of the main street in the village.

The castle stands at the top of a slope down to the River Strule, and was built between 1615 and 1619 by Sir Robert Newcomen; the associated lands and castle were sold to his son-in-law Sir William Stewart at the end of the following decade.

Parkanaur Manor House

Located within Parkanaur Forest, signposted off the A4 Dungannon to Ballygawley Road, the manor house was initially a three-gabled dwelling built in 1802 and owned by the Burges family. There were later additions in 1815 by Thomas Duff who created a large Elizabethan-style house.

Later that century, the house and adjoining garden were enhanced: gate lodges were added and thousands of trees planted. The interior contains a great hall and minstrels' gallery.

Roughan Castle
This small castle located near the village of Newmills and south-west of Roughan Lough, was possibly erected by Andrew Stewart around 1618. Three storeys high, it consists of a central square tower with stout rounded towers at each corner. It later belonged to Sir Phelim O'Neill who was captured on a nearby crannóg in 1653 and hanged in Dublin.

Killymoon Castle
Located in the town of Cookstown, this castle is sited on a raised north terrace slope overlooking the Ballinderry river. It was first built in 1671 by James Stewart, and rebuilt in 1803 by Colonel William Stewart from a design by the famous English architect John Nash.

The south front of the castle has a large circular tower nearly at its centre with slim taller attached tower behind this. The parkland of the castle is now a spectacular golf course. The castle and grounds are private, and arrangements to view the castle can be made by appointment – it is a popular venue for newly weds who book the castle and its grounds for family photographs.

Lissan House
Lissan House lies on the outskirts of Cookstown. It is a huge structure of enormous historical significance set within a 250-acre demesne of ancient woodland and forestry, which was created in the seventeenth century. It was, until the death of its last resident, Hazel Radclyffe Dolling, the oldest domestic dwelling in Ireland continually inhabited by one family.

Inside, the most striking feature is the large oak staircase which rises from the stone-flagged entrance hall the full height of the building. The other most notable feature of the house is its octagonal ballroom, added by Sir Thomas Staples around 1830 with its fine, restrained neo-classical plasterwork, Dublin chimneypiece and carved door frames.

Lissan House reached the final of the BBC Restoration programme in 2003. It is open to the public for tours, and has modern interactive exhibits. It should be pointed out that while the house itself is located in County Tyrone, some of its grounds are based in County Derry!

Loughry House
Close to Tullahogue Fort stood Loughry House where Dean Jonathan Swift occasionally stayed with the Lindsay family. It is thought he wrote his satirical works such as, 'A Modest Proposal' at this venue. Nowadays Loughry College – a renowned agricultural college – is based here.

Blessingbourne House

This large manor house is situated in an impressive 550-acre country estate nestled in the heart of woodlands and wildlife on the edge of the Clogher Valley near Fivemiletown, and was constructed between 1870 and 1874.

It originally came to the Montgomery family in the early years of the eighteenth century. Nowadays the estate is a working farm and has a popular bike trail as well as a Carriage and Costume Museum – which comprises a unique collection of original carriages and Victorian costumes from the manor house.

FORESTS IN TYRONE

There are thirty forests located throughout County Tyrone, ranging in size from 100 acres (Castlederg Forest) to larger forest parks such as Gortin Glen Forest Park which encompasses 3,790 acres.

Davagh Forest

Ten miles north-west of Cookstown, Davagh Forest covers 3,700 acres. The forest is largely upland coniferous set in the foothills of the Sperrins, and has a series of casual trails. The public are welcome to visit this forest on foot, and try to catch a glimpse of the sika deer.

Alternatively, 2013 saw the official opening of the Davagh Forest Trails – incorporating a skills park and pump track attracting thousands of mountain bikers each month.

Gortin Glen Forest Park

This forest is situated on the main road between Gortin and Omagh, and was originally planted solely for timber production. The forest park opened in 1967, embracing 3,790 acres of ground. It was the first forest park to be established in purely coniferous woodland. The park itself provides a stunning gateway to the Sperrin Mountains and Gortin Lakes, with three waymarked nature trails and the 5-mile designated car trek, which offers some breathtaking views of the countryside.

Drum Manor Forest Park

Its close proximity to Cookstown (3 miles) makes it an attractive venue for tourists. Drum Manor was acquired from Archibald Close by the Forest Service in 1964 and opened to the public as a forest park in 1970, having originally been an eighteenth-century demesne. It is colourful in spring and autumn with shrub, butterfly and Japanese gardens, ponds and waymarked trails among its many attractions.

Favour Royal Forest Park

Located just off the main Augher to Aughnacloy Road, the Ulster Way passes through this forest. There is also a wildflower meadow and deer lawn, which can be accessed from the Favour Royal car park. Altadavin car park is located beside St Patrick's Chair and St Brigid's Well.

MOUNTAINS AND GLENS IN TYRONE

Apart from the Sperrin Mountains, there are other notable mountains and glens based (or at least partly based) in Tyrone, such as Slieve Beagh and the Mountains of Pomeroy.

Sperrins

The Sperrins region is a designated 'Area of Outstanding Natural Beauty', popular with hill-walkers and explorers. The wider Sperrins area stretches from the Donegal border in the west, to Lough Neagh in the east, taking in a large part of eastern Tyrone.

The range lies between the Tyrone towns Omagh, Cookstown and Strabane and is about 40 miles from east to west. Four scenic driving routes have been created in the Sperrins area: the Central, South, East and North Sperrins scenic routes.

The tallest peak in the Sperrins is Mount Sawel. While there are ten summits over 500 yards above sea level, at 741 yards Mount Sawel is one of the central peaks of an impressive range of Sperrin Mountains that straddles and marks the Tyrone-Derry boundary.

With cycling so popular in County Tyrone, it is no surprise that the Sperrins possess a superb network of signed cycle routes. The more experienced cyclist can take the 31-mile Gold Cycle Route, which passes along the ancient valleys of the Sperrins. Meanwhile motorists can experience one of the Sperrins' four scenic driving routes – these were included in National Geographic's list of the top scenic drives for 2012.

Sloughan Glen

This pleasant woodland walk near Drumquin takes the visitor steadily upwards to be greeted by the roar of its waterfall thundering over a rocky edge.

Sliabh Beagh

This mountainous area straddles the border between Counties Fermanagh, Monaghan and Tyrone – and the Sliabh Beagh Way is a 25-mile walk that actually begins at St Patrick's Chair and Well.

Mountains of Pomeroy

These are a small range of hills that run west of the town of Pomeroy – and this mountain range is well noted for being the subject of a ballad 'The Mountains of Pomeroy' by Dr George Sigerson.

RIVERS IN TYRONE

Rivers in County Tyrone include the Ballinderry, Blackwater, Derg, Strule, Mourne, Glenelly, Owenreagh, Owenkillew and Torrent. These all either feed into other rivers or into Lough Neagh.

River Strule

The Strule forms at the confluence of the Drumragh and Camowen rivers in the centre of Omagh. It runs northwards for 12 miles, bounded by rich pasture and occasional cereal crops. Along its length it is joined by the Fairy Water and the Owenkillew before meeting the Derg below Newtownstewart to form the River Mourne.

River Mourne

The Mourne is a mere 10 miles long, running from Newtownstewart to Lifford Bridge. The tributaries which feed into the Mourne include the River Derg, the River Cavanalee, the Douglas Burn, and the Grevenue Burn.

River Derg

The Derg has its source high in the Donegal hills, flowing out of the lough of the same name to join with the River Strule and form the Mourne downstream of Newtownstewart. The upper reaches are mountainous while the lower stretches flow through pasture and cereal fields.

River Owenreagh and River Owenkillew

The Owenreagh and Owenkillew rise in the Sperrin Mountains and flow westwards, forming part of the Foyle system. They are notable for the physical diversity of the banks and channels and the richness and naturalness of its plant and animal communities.

River Ballinderry

The Ballinderry rises at 230 yards in a small lough called Camlough, nestled between the peaks of Evishanoran and Craignagore Mountains, on the southern slopes of the Sperrin Mountain range. Leaving Camlough the river begins a 30-mile long journey, flowing northward for a few miles before turning east towards Cookstown and Coagh and reaching its journey's end on the western shore of Lough Neagh.

River Blackwater
The Blackwater flows in County Armagh and County Tyrone, as well as County Monaghan, which has its source to the north of Fivemiletown in Tyrone. The river acts as a natural division between the three counties.

LOUGHS IN TYRONE

Lough Neagh is the largest lake in Ireland or Britain (and fifth largest in Europe) – Counties Down, Armagh, Antrim, Derry and Tyrone all have shores on the lough and it covers a total area of 160 square miles. The name Lough Neagh means 'the Lough of the horse-god Eochu'. Approximately 19 miles long and 10 miles wide, it contains several islands such as Coney Island close to the County Tyrone shoreline. A Loughshore Cycle Trail forms a continuous 128-mile cycle route around the shores of Lough Neagh, taking in many areas along the loughshore region of East Tyrone.

The Fishing Rights of Lough Neagh were disputed for four centuries – and the struggle in which the fishermen were eventually victorious in the early 1970s had been bitter and protracted.

It was a Member of Parliament for Cork in the Westminster Parliament, Tim Healy, later the first Governor General of the Irish Free State, who researched and wrote a comprehensive book on the subject in 1913 – *Stolen Waters*.

There are numerous other loughs dotted around the county – including Lough Bradan near Omagh (popular with anglers); Roughan Lough near Coalisland; while Ballysaggart Lough is also known as the 'Black Lough' and is located at the edge of the town of Dungannon. It is part of the system of lakes and waterways that were built to service the Moygashel mills.

Another Lough of interest is situated along the border with County Derry: Lough Fea is set in wild mountain scenery on the south-west slope of Slieve Gallion – located midway between Cookstown and Draperstown. Covering 180 acres, the lough has a 2.5 miles relatively flat walkway that is popular with visitors.

NATIONAL TRUST PROPERTIES

The National Trust protects historic houses, gardens, mills and many other important visitor attractions based in Tyrone and its surrounding counties. There are two properties that the organisation is responsible for in County Tyrone.

Wellbrook Beetling Mill

This mill is located in Kildress, just off the main Cookstown to Omagh Road, and is nestled in a beautiful wooded valley. Visitors can experience the different processes of linen making as a cottage industry of the nineteenth century: beetling was the last stage in the manufacturing of linen.

The rush of the river drives the 16ft wheel powered by the nearby Ballinderry river, and the beetles speed up, clattering and hammering and breaking the silence: it is the last surviving beetling mill of its kind in Northern Ireland.

Gray's Printing Press

This treasure trove of history tells the story of ink, galleys, presses and ultimately emigration in the eighteenth-century printing press where John Dunlap, printer of the American Declaration of Independence (see Chapter 6) and James Wilson, grandfather of President Woodrow Wilson, may possibly have learned their trade. Behind the eighteenth-century shopfront in the heart of Strabane, visitors can step back in time and hear the story of printing.

3

TYRONE TOWNS, VILLAGES AND TOWNLANDS: FACTS AND STATISTICS

Tyrone remains a largely rural county, but it does have a diverse range of towns and villages to service the rural population. The four largest towns are surrounded by a network of smaller settlements and outlying areas of population, with areas of south-east Tyrone (particularly around the Cookstown and Dungannon areas) consisting of many medium and small villages.

Omagh, the county town of Tyrone, is one such example. This is recorded by the 2011 census as being the only 'large' town in the county (with a population between 18,000 and 75,000) – and is central to villages such as Beragh, Drumquin and Killyclogher.

The three 'medium' towns as designated by the most recent census figures (population between 10,000 and 18,000) are: Cookstown, Dungannon and Strabane – and along with Omagh all currently have district councils of their own.

This, however, is anticipated to change during April 2015 with the scheduled implementation of the local government reform that will incorporate major changes in the local political landscape within Tyrone and other neighbouring counties. Tyrone towns and villages are set to be included within the new 'supercouncils' of Derry and Strabane, Fermanagh and Omagh, and Mid-Ulster.

Smaller towns in County Tyrone include Coalisland and Castlederg, while among the many villages located around Tyrone are Augher, Donaghmore and Trillick. This chapter will look at the four largest towns in terms of population and also a selection of towns and villages based around their locality throughout Tyrone – focusing on their unique histories, traditions and characteristics.

LAND DIVISIONS IN COUNTY TYRONE PAST AND PRESENT

Barony: The barony is a now obsolete administrative unit that is midway in size between a county and a parish. They were created, like the county, in the centuries after the Norman invasion. Some early baronies were later subdivided into half baronies with the same standing as full baronies.

Parish: The present-day civil parish was once an ecclesiastical unit of territory based on early Christian and monastic settlements in Ireland. It came into existence in Ireland in the twelfth and thirteenth centuries, and was continued by the Church of Ireland after the reformation. It was later adopted as a civil administrative area. However, over time some civil and ecclesiastical boundaries came to vary. The boundaries of Church of Ireland parishes largely coincide with those of civil parishes and are called by the same name.

In contrast, Roman Catholic parishes, though originally based on what became the civil parish, frequently do not correspond with the names or boundaries of civil parishes. They are often made up of several civil parishes or parts of civil parishes.

Townland: The townland is the smallest administrative division of land throughout Ireland that is still in use. It was during the era of surveys and map-making of the plantation era, that the variety of small, local land units were given the general name of the townland.

In naming townlands, frequent use was made of natural or man-made features of the landscape and surnames of local families. In Tyrone the term has a special resonance with people; as a number of townlands form a parish, it helps to identify small local rural areas. Townlands can vary in size from a few acres to over 7,000 acres.

In *Townland Names of County Tyrone*, Patrick McAleer, the Irish Folklore Commission's representative until 1941, recorded each townland name in Tyrone – visiting each of them by bicycle – noting the topographical and geographical features which form the basis of the Gaelic name. He also concentrated on the local pronunciation of the townland names, which in many cases differed very much from their anglicised forms.

Some examples include:

Belnaclogh (*Beal na gCloch*) – Ford mouth of the stones
Donaghenry (*Domhnach Fhainre*) – Sloping church land
Ganvaghan (*Gain mheachan*) – Little sandy place
Kiltamnagh (*Coill Tamhnach*) – Wood of the green fields
Mullaghdaly (*Mullach Dala*) – Hill where meetings were held
Tattyclunagh (*Taite Cluaine*) – Division of the meadows
Drumshambo (*Droim Sean Bhoithe*) – Ridge of the old hut or tent
Cregganconroe (*Creagan Con Ruaidh*) – Little rock of the red hound (fox)

Diocese: The Church developed an administrative structure of dioceses, each being an area over which a bishop presided. Made up of groups of parishes, the boundaries of dioceses were largely settled by the fourteenth century. Most are named after important Church or monastic foundations, such as Clogher. The majority of County Tyrone is incorporated into either the dioceses of Armagh or Derry.

MAIN TOWNS AND THEIR LOCAL AREAS

Cookstown – An Cora Criche – *Round Hill of the Boundary*
Cookstown derives its (English) name from its founder, Dr Allen Cooke. An ecclesiastical lawyer, he had obtained leases of land in the vicinity of Tullyhogue and applied for, and was granted, a Royal Charter to form a market town, which was named after him. With the charter, free

commerce in buying and selling was granted. It also established one free market every Saturday – which continues to prosper.

The original town was built in about 1609, but was destroyed in the rebellion of 1641. The present town was built about 1750 by William Stewart of Killymoon. He had become interested in town planning as a result of schemes which he had seen being carried out in Dublin. Impressed by the wide thoroughfares in Edinburgh and Dublin, Stewart instructed his surveyor to plan a new town with an avenue that would rival those in these cities.

As a result, Cookstown has the distinction of having one of the longest and widest streets in Ireland. The Main Street stretches to over 1.25 miles long (in a straight line) and is up to 135ft wide in places.

It was due to this statistic that Cookstown became known as 'Long Hungry Cookstown' soon after reconstruction, and was one of the main centres of the linen industry in Tyrone. By 1832, the frontages along the main street had been built up but the minor streets remained quiet country lanes.

Cookstown is a thriving town, and is proud of its local motto: 'Looking Good, Looking Great!' Along with its town centre, it possesses a number of retail developments on the edge of town. The town also hosts impressive sporting and leisure amenities, such as the Burnavon Arts and Cultural Centre, and the Mid-Ulster Sports Arena.

Some of the smaller settlements in Cookstown area include:

Ardboe – Ard Bó – *Height of the Cows*
Ardboe is an area of historical importance in East Tyrone, with the Old Cross a prominent feature. The area has a strong cultural identity, as can be seen in the local Kinturk centre which celebrates the tradition of fishing in Lough Neagh. The Auld Lammas Fair is a popular event held each August in Ardboe, attracting hundreds of people of all ages.

Coagh – An Uaich – *A Low-lying Hollow Place*
Coagh is a small village situated on a ford on the Ballinderry river. The village was founded by George Butler Conyngham in 1724. The name 'Coagh' derives from the Irish *An Uaich* meaning 'The Hollow' and is

appropriate given that the village nestles amidst low-lying land between the Sperrins and Lough Neagh.

Greencastle – An Caisleain Glás
Greencastle is a crossroads village off the Omagh to Cookstown road. Close by is the picturesque Cashel Bridge which crosses the upper reaches of the Owenreagh river. In the surrounding areas there are many interesting places to visit, such as *An Creagán*, Beaghmore Stone Circles, Cashel House and Glenhull.

Kildress – Cill Dreasa – *Church of Brambles*
Kildress is a rural parish resting peacefully at the foot of the Sperrin Mountains. It has a scattered population and is an area with some breathtaking scenery, with Beaghmore Stone Circles arguably the most prominent feature. It is considered to be the only maintained stone-circle site amongst nearly 150 in the Sperrin Hills. The main route of the popular Cookstown 100 Motorbike Race is situated in Kildress.

Pomeroy – Cabhán an Chaorthainn – *Round Hill of the Mountain Ash*
Pomeroy is located in the foothills of the Sperrins, 10 miles from both Cookstown and Dungannon. It is part of an area consisting of an oak forest granted to Sir Andrew Chichester by King James I. It is the highest village in Tyrone (564ft above sea level) and was planned by Revd James Lowry in the eighteenth century. The village has a central square, situated at the top of a steep hill.

Rock – An Charraig
Rock, or 'The Rock' as many local people prefer to call it, is a small rural village situated 6 miles from Cookstown and 8 miles from Dungannon. The focal point for the area is the village square, with a number of shops located in it. The nearby Tullylagan Manor covers approximately 30 acres; the original mansion dates to 1832.

Stewartstown – An Chraobh – *The Branch or Wooded Land*
This area was known as *An Chraobh* before the plantation and it was on the crannóg in Crieve Lough that Hugh O'Neill, Earl of Tyrone, spent his last night in Ireland before setting sail from Rathmullan, County Donegal in September 1607 (see Flight of the Earls, Chapter 1).

The village of Stewartstown was built by Andrew Stewart, 3rd Lord Stewart of Ochiltree, 1st Lord Castlestewart. In 1611 he settled in Ulster, where he was granted 3,000 acres in County Tyrone. He built his house overlooking Crieve Lough during this time.

Stewartstown became a popular market town during the nineteenth century and this was helped with the opening of Stewartstown railway station on 28 July 1879. This lasted for almost eighty years – closing on 1 June 1958.

Tullaghoge – Tullach Óg – *The Little Hill of Youth*

Tullaghoge is a small village situated between Cookstown and Stewartstown in East Tyrone. It is an area steeped in history, and the name is derived from the Irish *Tullach Óg* meaning 'The Little Hill of Youth'. A new project to establish a training facility for the Police Service of Northern Ireland will be based in nearby Desertcreat.

DUNGANNON – *DÚN GEANAINN* – 'GEANANN'S HILLFORT'

The history of Dungannon is one that is very much intertwined with the history of County Tyrone, as many of the key events that have happened within South or East Tyrone have happened or originated in the Dungannon area.

According to legend, Dungannon was named from Geanann, a Red Branch Knight and a son of Cathbad the chief Ulster druid, who dwelt in the palace of Eamain Macha, with their king, Concobar Mac Nessa. Geanann's fort was situated above the present Market Square on high ground.

The O'Neills took up residence in Dungannon during the fourteenth century, having moved from the drystone fort of the Grianan above Derry. O'Neills Castle is situated where Geanann had his fort; the Annals of the Four Masters record that Hugh O'Donnell of Donegal led an army into Tyrone and demolished the old castle.

Though it had been O'Neill's capital with its own developed social code and high level of learning, the concept of a 'town' had been no more than a collection of huts draped around Castle Hill. However, in 1609 it became a planned municipality with its Market Square, Scotch Street and Irish Street.

It was awarded a charter in 1612 with a governing body of mayor (sovereign) and twelve burgesses (mostly members of the Chichester family); and a Royal School was also founded by charter in 1614 by James I to ensure 'that there shall be one Free School at least appointed in every County, for the education of youth in learning and religion'.

The native population was highly resistant to these changes, and in 1641 Sir Phelim O'Neill gave the signal for rebellion one evening as he was dining at Charlemont Fort. In one night, the fortress, together with Dungannon and Mountjoy, were destroyed.

By 1692, Thomas Knox had purchased the town, and the boundaries of the Dungannon township expanded rapidly. The boom years of the domestic linen industry were roughly between 1775 and 1825. This era coincided with momentous events in the sphere of politics, such as the 'Dungannon Convention'.

In 1782–3 this Volunteer Convention met in the town (see Chapter 1) and, along with the importance of its status as a linen centre, so much progress was being made in rebuilding the town that by 1802 John McEvoy described it as: 'one of the most prosperous towns in the north of Ireland in the linen trade, nor is it inferior to any other for its rapid progress in building.'

The Ulster Railway reached Dungannon in 1858, and six years later the Dickson family installed the first power looms in Dungannon and subsequently the Stevensons opened their Moygashel factory. Since that time, expansion and change in Dungannon has been rapid and impressive.

Old industries have made way for new, and the railway has been replaced by a motorway as the main channel of transport to other places in Tyrone and neighbouring Ulster counties. The new cultural, recreational and sporting facilities that have been established since the mid-twentieth century have coincided with a high percentage of migrant workers from other countries.

Some of the smaller settlements in Dungannon area include:

Augher – An Eochair – *The Edge/Border*
Augher is a busy community in the Clogher Valley, based on the Blackwater river. Gollagh Woods, which border the river on the east side of Augher, are a noted beauty spot.

Spur Royal Castle is situated just outside the village; this is a plantation castle built in 1615 on the site of an older fortress. It was burned in 1689 but restored and extended in 1832, and the building now forms an impressive structure overlooking a tree-edged lake. To the north side of the village are hills that reach 779ft at the craggy ridge of Knockmany.

Aughnacloy – Achadh na Cloiche – *Field of the Stones*
Aughnacloy was created as a town under the 1854 Town Improvements Act. It is located along the Blackwater's banks near the border with Monaghan, and is an excellent walking and touring centre; those interested in railways will be keen to see the station that was once the headquarters of the Clogher Valley Railway, one of the most notable of Ireland's narrow-gauge lines. Nearby Lismore is the site of a large bawn with corner towers – built by Sir Thomas Ridgeway in 1611.

Ballygawley – Baile Uí Dhálaigh – *O'Daly's Town*
A few miles north-west of Aughnacloy is Ballygawley. There was a time when a popular market and livestock fair was held in the main street. In the local area is *Sess Kilgreen*, a fine chambered tomb of a kind

found throughout Western Europe between 3,000 and 1,000 BC. West of Ballygawley village at Errigal Keerogue, are the ruins of St Kiernan's Church with its very early cross.

Benburb – An Beann Bhorb – *Proud or Bold Cliff*
Situated on the border with Armagh, Benburb is a small village that lies above the Benburb Valley, stretching for over a mile from Milltown to Maydown Bridge. Benburb is best known in historical terms for the Battle of Benburb that took place in 1646, a battle that saw Munro's Scottish Army defeated by the troops of Owen Roe O'Neill at the townland of Drumflugh, a mile outside the village.

Brocagh – An Brocach – *The Place of the Badgers*
Brocagh is a thriving community on the western shore of Lough Neagh, approximately 4 miles from Coalisland. The nearby ruins of Mountjoy Castle still stand on the shore of Lough Neagh, while John Canavan was a local poet of renown during the late nineteenth and early twentieth centuries.

Caledon – Cionn Aird – *High Head*
Situated in the south-east of Tyrone and on the border of both Counties Armagh and Monaghan, Caledon (formerly known as Kinnaird) is a designated conservation area located on the banks of the Blackwater river. Caledon House was built in 1779 by James Alexander, a member of the Irish House of Commons for Londonderry, who had previously bought the Caledon Estate in 1778.

Cappagh – An Cheapóg – *Land Cleared of Trees*
Situated in a central area of South Tyrone, the village and surrounding area, which includes Galbally, incorporates the townland of Altmore. The Altmore river is extremely popular for fishing. Cappagh village has developed since the seventeenth century. General James Shields, a former United States senator, was born there, while Shane Bearnagh the highwayman also hailed from the district.

Castlecaulfield – Baile Uí Dhonnghaile – *Donnelly's Townland*
This village is situated 3 miles west of Dungannon and was formerly known as 'Ballydonnelly' after the Irish *Baile Uí Dhonnghaile*. Castlecaulfield Horticultural Show is held each August in the village; the show was first staged in 1954 and has grown to be one of the biggest of its kind in Ireland. Parkanaur Forest is also situated close to the village.

Coalisland – Oileán an Ghuail

Coalisland was one of the earliest industrial communities in Ulster and was once the terminus of a busy canal (constructed in 1733) that conveyed coal and other traffic to and from Belfast and Dublin, but was closed down in 1946. The Torrent river, a great source of industrial water power, is also a beautiful natural feature. Former World Snooker Champion Dennis Taylor hails from the town.

Clogher – An Cloch Óir – *Golden Stone/Stony Place*

Clogher is a village at the confluence of the Fury and Blackwater rivers. It is one of the most ancient settlements in Ireland, and one with a very fair share of historic buildings and other features. The main street climbs upwards to its eighteenth-century Church of Ireland Cathedral. The village can claim the oldest bishopric in Ireland – its first bishop was St MacCartan, a disciple of St Patrick.

Donaghmore – Domhnach Mór – *Great Church*

The small village of Donaghmore is situated a few miles from Dungannon, and is the place where St Patrick is said to have founded a religious establishment in the fifth century AD. An Early Christian bronze bell associated with Donaghmore parish is kept in the National Museum, Dublin. Standing impressively in the village is the large Celtic cross. The Old National School (built in 1885) has been converted into a Heritage Centre for the local area.

Edendork – Éadan na dTorc – *Hill Brow of the Hogs*

Edendork is an area situated between Dungannon and Coalisland in East Tyrone. Although predominantly rural, there have been a number of important industries located here, including Tyrone Crystal which was based in Edendork for a number of years. It is a centre of historical importance, with the first Civil Rights march having proceeded through the area.

Eglish – An Eaglais – *The Church*

Eglish is a small village whose close neighbours include Benburb and Moy, each only a few miles away. The focal point of the community is the Gaelic Athletic Association complex, incorporating a playing pitch and hall. The heads of two high crosses have been mounted on modern shafts in a hilltop graveyard on the outskirts of Eglish village.

Fivemiletown – Baile na Lorgan – *Town on the Long Ridge*

Fivemiletown stands on a long hilltop ridge close to the Fermanagh border – and indeed, its former name, *Baile na Lorgan*, means 'town on the long ridge'. The present name derives from the town's location 5 Irish miles* from its nearest neighbours of Clogher and also Brookeborough and Tempo in County Fermanagh. Established as a 'plantation' town, Fivemiletown is noted for its large creamery that was established by H.D. Montgomery in 1898.

Moy – An Maigh – *Level Land*
The village of Moy is located several miles south-east of Dungannon on the Blackwater river, which here forms the county border with Armagh. With a large square as its focal point, Moy was founded as a plantation settlement in 1764 by Lord Charlemont. For many years Moy was the site of one of Ireland's most famous horse fairs.

Newmills
The River Torrent runs through this small village in East Tyrone and while it is in close proximity to both Coalisland and Dungannon, it derived its own name from a corn mill and kilns which formerly stood in the area. The nearby Annaginny Fisheries is a stocked and managed lake with fish guaranteed for the visitor, while Roughan Castle and Lough is only a mile from the village.

OMAGH – *AN ÓMAIGH* – 'THE UNTILLED PLAIN' OR 'SEAT OF THE CHIEFS'

The history of Omagh stretches back over 1,000 years. It originated as a tiny settlement situated at the point where the rivers Camowen and Drumragh flow together to form the River Strule. According to legend (fire and battle have destroyed most of the ancient documents and records) the town is said to owe its origin to a monastic abbey founded in 792. In the same year it is said that Flaithgel, son of Taichloch, abbot of Drumragh, died.

The abbey is reported as being converted into a house for the Third Order of the Franciscans in 1464, and continued to flourish as such until the dissolution of the monastery, when its site and possessions were granted to Sir Henry Piers.

Omagh had began to develop a reputation as a fortress town by the middle of the fifteenth century, when the occupant of the castle was Art O'Neill. It was around 1470 when Henry O'Neill, King of Ulster, with his headquarters at Dungannon, captured the Omagh castle from Art and handed it over to his eldest son and heir, Conn Mór.

With the Plantation of Ulster in 1609, Omagh was granted to Lord

---

*An Irish mile is 2,240 yards while an English one is only 1,760 yards!

Castlehaven, but he failed to erect a castle or settle a sufficient number of English in the area – so the town and district were given to Captain Edmund Leigh and his brothers John and Daniel.

Leigh's fort is believed to have been built on a hill overlooking the Derry Road. Charles I granted the manor of Arleston or Audleston, north of Omagh and comprising 2,000 acres, to James Mervyn in 1631; exactly a decade later Phelim O'Neill is said to have marched against the Castle of Omagh.

Most of the town of Omagh was destroyed by fire in 1742, but it recovered and by 1768, Omagh had replaced Dungannon as the county town of County Tyrone. Like Strabane, Omagh has depended on the construction of bridges to facilitate trade: the King James Bridge over the Drumragh river, so called because it is said that King James passed over it, still stands from the seventeenth century; 1840 saw the erection of Donnelly's Bridge on the Killyclogher Road; Bell's Bridge was constructed in the early nineteenth century; Abbey Bridge in 1900, the Drumragh Bridge in 1966 and the most recent, the Steel Bow Arch pedestrian and cycle bridge that weighs 60 tonnes and spans 58 metres across the River Strule. This bridge was opened in July 2014.

The terrible events of Saturday, 15 August 1998 will never be forgotten, and the site of the explosion is marked by a pillar, made of 6 tonnes of ultra-clear 'laboratory' glass, 4.5m high. Near the top, inside appears a three-dimensional 'heart' in a faceted cut-glass style. The suggested image is that of the heart suspended high in a frozen beam of light, representing love and the nearby memorial garden, about 300 yards away, has thirty-one pole-mounted small mirrors, one for each life lost. The idea is a gesture towards redeeming human values in the face of the atrocity.

Omagh is currently the most populated town in Tyrone (approximately 25,000 people), and is the key focal point in Mid- and West Tyrone with its impressive range of facilities. The Omagh through-pass opened in August 2006, while Omagh town centre is dominated by its classical-styled courthouse, from behind which rise the gothic-styled spires of the local churches. Some of the smaller settlements in the Omagh area include:

Beragh – An Bearach – *The Place of Birch Trees*

Beragh is a small village approximately 8 miles from Omagh. One of the first references to the village was on a plantation map of Ireland of 1609, where it had a market patent granted under the name 'Lowrystown'.

Donaghanie contains the ruins of an old church said to have been founded by St Patrick in the fifth century. A stone at the house bears what is supposed to be the mark of St Patrick's knee. One vault in the graveyard contains an inscription saying that it must not be opened until the day of resurrection or after.

Carrickmore – An Charraig Mhór – *The Big Rock*

The town of Carrickmore is about 10 miles east of Omagh and is situated on an elevated site called 'The Rock' by local people. The original name of the village came from the Irish '*An Charraig Mhór*' which means 'Big Rock'. The area was once known as Termonmaguirke owing to the Maguirc clan becoming stewards of the church lands after battles fought between the various clans.

It is steeped in history and there are many tales and legends connected with St Colmcille and the town. A wide range of historic monuments can be found in the Carrickmore area such as cairns, stone circles, standing stones and raths. The college in Carrickmore is named after Dean Brian Maguirc, a famous priest of the Maguirc (McGurk) family who was Vicar-General to St Oliver Plunkett around the year 1700. An important event in the town each year is the Mid-Ulster Drama Festival which attracts participants and visitors from many parts of Ireland to the popular Patrician Hall venue.

Dromore – An Droim Mór – *The Great Ridge*

The town of Dromore is located 9 miles south-west of Omagh in West Tyrone. The name originates from the Irish *An Droim Mór*, meaning 'The Great Ridge'. There are many hills in the area, and the heather-clad *Greenan* is tall enough to dominate the whole parish.

William Hamilton established the town in 1757; and the name of the townland in which it is sited – 'Mullinacross' – is derived from an ancient stone cross that stood at the top of the large hill overlooking the town. Hills dominate the local landscape – and the largest, Greenan, is 864ft tall.

Drumquin – Droim Caoin – *Pleasant Ridge*

The village of Drumquin is located 6 miles west of Omagh, and sits on the Drumquin river – also known as the 'Fairy Water' – one of the tributaries of the Foyle catchment area. The area contains some of the most beautiful and scenic sights to be found in County Tyrone, including the nearby Dooish Mountain.

Fintona – Fionntamhnach – *The Fair-Coloured Field or Land*

Situated around 8 miles south of Omagh, Fintona and its hinterland is thought to have had human habitation for around 4,000 years and there are numerous examples of burial places, standing stones, stone circles and Bronze Age pottery in the area.

The O'Neills built a fortress here in the fifteenth century, but eventually the town passed in 1668 into the possession of the Eccles family. The town is strongly linked with the equestrian tradition and the Ecclesville Equestrian Centre provides a range of equestrian-related sports.

Gortin – An Goirtín – *Little Enclosed Field*
Gortin lies 10 miles north of Omagh in the valley of the Owenkillew river, overlooked by the Munterlunny mountains. The scenic road from Omagh, which traverses Gortin Gap, passes between Mullaghcarn (1,778ft) and Curraghchosaly (1,372ft) Its small, rural population lives in a village that, while dependent on agriculture for its economy, has also developed the tourism potential of this area of rugged beauty and tranquillity. Tourist attractions in the area include the Gortin Glen Forest Park.

Killyclogher – Coill an Clochar – *Wood of the Stone Structure/ Mountfield* – Achadh Ard – *High Field*
This is a large village in Mid-Tyrone on the outskirts of the county town of Omagh, and includes the large townland of Mountfield to the south. Sir William McMahon developed these areas in the early nineteenth century. The 1041ft Muldreg Hill rises above Mountfield.

Loughmacrory – Loch Mhic Ruairí
A small village located 3 miles from Carrickmore, it is characterised by its ancient landmarks such as the Loughmacrory Wedge Tomb. It has a close community spirit that has been strengthened by having its own Gaelic football team since the early 1970s. The sport of handball is also quite popular in the area.

Seskinore – Seisceann Odhar – *Pale Grey Marshy Bog*
Seskinore is a quiet village situated 7 miles from Omagh. In 1662, a Welshman named James Perry obtained a grant of the lands of Mullaghmore and named it Perrymount. Seskinore village was built in the immediate neighbourhood.

Sixmilecross – Na Corracha Móra – *The Round Hills*
Sixmilecross is a small village located 6 Irish miles from Omagh – hence its anglicised name. The cross is said to be derived from a Celtic cross that stood in a field outside of the village, in the townland of Aughnaglea. The village was established in 1634, and the manor and surrounding lands all belonged to the Earl of Belmore.

Trillick – Trí Leac – *Three Remarkable Stones*
Trillick is a village in south-west Tyrone situated on the border with County Fermanagh. The name is derived from the Irish *Trí Leac* meaning 'three remarkable stones', another term for a chambered tomb. In the seventh century, Trillick had an abbey, and it is thought that the O'Neills, who owned the land, had a fort in the area. In the seventeenth-century plantation, the Trillick area was passed to the Mervyn family who proceeded to build a castle in the north of the village, the remains of which can be seen today.

STRABANE – *AN TSRATH BÁN* – THE WHITE STRAND OR FAIR HOLM

The name Strabane is derived from *An tSrath Bán* which comes directly from the reference to the River Mourne, meaning the White Strand or Fair Holm. It is the most northerly district in Tyrone and is divided from Lifford in County Donegal by the River Finn.

There have been three different castles in Strabane, all subsequently destroyed. These have represented three different periods in history during which Strabane had a settled community with a castle as a fortification. One of these is believed to have belonged to Turlough Lynagh O'Neill, who had a centre of power in Strabane. Each castle was believed to have stood within easy reach of the River Mourne.

James Hamilton, the Earl of Abercorn, came to Strabane as the Jacobean grantee, and his castle was built in 1609 – interestingly his family were Roman Catholic in an era when the vast majority of planters were Protestant. The earl proceeded to build the town which in 1612 became a borough, and sent two Members to the Parliament in Dublin.

During the 1641 rebellion, the town was burnt. It was from 1708 that Strabane began to enjoy the prosperity of the linen trade. Printing and publishing also flourished in Strabane; fifty books were printed in Strabane between 1779 and 1840.

The earliest record of a bridge construction in this area was over the River Foyle from Strabane to Lifford in 1743. Another bridge was built over the Mourne in 1788 which was an indication of the development of the town. This replaced the ferry service over the river and marked the opening of the permanent route of communications to the south of the town. The bridge had to be widened in 1823 due to the increase in commercial traffic and the improvement in transport.

The town suffered a devastating flood on 22 October 1987 when the River Mourne burst its banks, leaving homes and businesses destroyed. The flooding started in the Lower Main Street and Railway Street areas and quickly spread to other parts of the town centre, leaving much of it partially submerged. At its height, there was up to 4ft of water in Abercorn Square.

Strabane is noted for its many famous cultural associations including the fiction writer Flann O'Brien, the hymn writer Cecil Frances Alexander – of 'All Things Bright and Beautiful' fame – and John Dunlap, printer of the American Declaration of Independence.

Some of the smaller settlements in Strabane area include:

Artigarvan – Ard Ti Garbhain – *The Height of Garbhan's House*
Located about 2 miles north of Strabane, Artigarvan is a small village on the banks of the Glenmornan river. The river was once a source of power for a cornmill, a paper mill and a spade factory. While these have

now gone, one of the waterwheels, though not in use, is kept in good condition as it was one of the largest in Ireland – 20ft in diameter.

Castlederg – Caisleán na Deirge – *Castle on the River Derg*

Located in the north-west corner of Tyrone, Castlederg is close to the border with Donegal. Two ancient tombs exist in the area – known as the 'Druid's Altar' and 'Todd's Den'. In historical terms, Castlederg was first mentioned at the end of the fifteenth century when the Annals of the Four Masters identified a castle along the banks of the River Derg.

Clady – An Cladigh – *Muddy Margin of a Stream or a River*

A small village located on the border with Donegal, Clady village is surrounded by beautiful rolling countryside. The area is also known by many people as 'Urney' after the name of the parish. It has long been associated with St Columba. Carricklee House is a magnificent building that stands in 5 acres of mature gardens overlooking the Finn river. It was built around 1780.

Donemana – Dún na Manach – *Fortress of the Monks*

Donemana is a small market village situated on the Burndennet river and nestling at the foothills of the Sperrin Mountain Range. The village was established in the early seventeenth century as part of the Ulster Plantation.

Sir John Drummond was granted 1,000 acres of land, and in establishing the village he also built a water mill for grinding corn on the river, which can be viewed on the outskirts of the village at the Silverbrook Mill Complex.

Killeter – Coill Íochtair – *Lower Wood*

Killeter is a small village in North Tyrone that is situated in the heart of the Derg Valley. The name of the general area is known by local people as 'Aghyaran'. The present St Patrick's Church of Ireland parish church (known locally as Badoney Church) was built in 1784 and is thought to occupy the site of an early Christian monastery.

Newtownstewart – An Baile Nua

Overlooked by hills called Bessy Bell and Mary Gray, and at the confluence of the rivers Strule and Owenkillew, the townland of Newtownstewart was historically called *Lislas*. It gained its current name when the land was granted to Sir William Stewart as part of the Plantation of Ulster.

Three miles to the south-west lies Baronscourt, the country seat of the Duke of Abercorn. With its neo-classical mansion and ornate Italian style gardens, it has been the home of the Duke of Abercorn's family since 1612. It also features an 18-hole golf course in the estate.

The lands around Newtownstewart were granted to a James Clapham but were soon sold to Sir Robert Newcomen. Under the plantation scheme new landowners were required to build a castle on their estate. Newcomen began work in 1615 and by 1622 the castle was described as '... a castle of lime and stone, 4 stories high. Around it is a Bawn of lime and stone, 81 feet long, 66 feet long and 9 feet high, with 2 flankers.'

In 1629 the lands and castle were sold to Sir William Stewart, of Newtown Stewart in Galloway, Scotland, who renamed the town after his family and birthplace.

Plumbridge

Plumbridge is a crossroads village, standing on the banks of the Glenelly river. Most of the village is on the northern bank of the Glenelly river, within the townland of Glencoppogagh. However, some of it lies on the southern bank, within the townland of Lisnacreaght.

Sion Mills – Muilean an tSiáin

Sion Mills is situated close to the Donegal border, just a few miles south of Strabane. A pleasant tree-lined industrial village and designated conservation area, Sion Mills is particularly rich in architectural heritage.

Herdman's Mill was founded in 1835, and the village's plentiful water resource, which once sustained a still thriving linen industry, now hosts an idyllic riverside walk. Sion Mills also has a strong cricket tradition and was the venue for a celebrated moment in cricket history when the Irish team beat a West Indian touring team in July 1969.

4

TYRONE FOLKLORE, CURES, CUSTOMS AND SUPERSTITIONS

Like most Irish counties, Tyrone has had its fair share of folklore, cures, customs and superstitions. While this chapter outlines those superstitions that are unique to the county – such as salt being carried in the pockets of mourners at funerals as protection against evil – some of those that may have originated in Tyrone may have also been observed in neighbouring counties.

THE NATIONAL FOLKLORE COLLECTION, UCD

Formerly known as the Department of Irish Folklore at University College Dublin (UCD), this collection is Ireland's primary repository of traditional vernacular culture since the establishment of the Irish Folklore Commission in 1935. See further information at: www.ucd.ie/irishfolklore.

Tyrone has had a number of close connections with this esteemed research centre. One of the former members of the Department of Irish Folklore was from Drumquin – Dr Seamus O'Cathain. In the book *Tyrone Folk Quest*, the esteemed folklorist Michael J. Murphy from Dromintee in South Armagh outlined his experiences as he spent a number of years at Glenhull and the surrounding areas in mid-Tyrone from 1949–1952. It was there that he lived while gathering the customs and traditions of the local inhabitants on behalf of the university department.

STORYTELLERS

Some areas of Mid- and West Tyrone have a tradition of storytelling, similar to other parts of Ulster such as South Armagh and West Donegal. One of Tyrone's leading storytellers during the twentieth century was Francis Daniel McAleer, who lived in Glenhull. Many of his stories and recollections on rural traditions were recorded by Michael J. Murphy and have subsequently passed into the national folklore collection in UCD.

Another was Michael McCanny from Drumquin (known locally as the *seanchaí* of Clunahill). Dr O'Cathain recorded valuable information from him during the 1970s on a variety of topics, including hiring fairs, local cures and wake games. Some of this was broadcast on Raidio Éireann in Dr O'Cathain's folk programme.

THE TRADITION OF THE CÉILÍ HOUSE

This entailed visiting a house for storytelling or chatting, singing or dancing – known in Tyrone as 'céilídhing'. At least one house in each area was a céilí house, but they were more associated with the rural areas of the county.

Michael J. Murphy vividly describes this tradition in *Tyrone Folk Quest*. In his attempts to record the traditions of the local area in Glenhull, he invited people round to his house for a 'céilí':

His cap seemed to be on and off. I sat back and wrote as he talked. No one took the slightest notice of me: they were intent on McCullagh's words. He was enjoying having listeners as they enjoyed listening ... not once did he stop talking tradition: not folktales, but material in Community and historical categories.

THE GENTLEMAN WHO PAYS THE RENT

The Clogher writer William Carleton (see Chapter 8) was one of the first well-known 'custom-collectors', and in the early nineteenth century he wrote in *Traits and Stories of the Irish Peasantry* about Phil Purcel the 'pig driver'.

In Tyrone, as in other parts of Ireland over the centuries, the family pig was very important as they helped the farmer earn money to pay the rent – especially those who could not afford a cow. Carleton described the amazement of a visitor to Phil's father's homestead when, as they were sitting around the fire, an old pig came in through the door, walked over to a ladder that was leaning against the loft, climbed it and settled down for a sleep.

The father explained that the old pig was very wise and very clean. When it slept, as it often did, near the fire with the occupant of the outshot bed, it always stayed on the side of the bed away from the wall, so if it wanted to go to the toilet in the middle of the night it could get out without disturbing anyone.

Apparently that pig had sired many fine piglets and Phil's father expressed that no one had a greater right in the house than 'the gentleman who paid the rent'. A pig that was house trained in those days was referred to as an 'educated pig'.

THE CHURCH OF THE HORSE

Around Beragh there was a legend as to the origin of Donaghanie Church or 'The Church of the Horse'. It is claimed that as St Patrick was walking towards the area he was stopped by a man with a horse and warned not to go further on account of the *peist* (monster).

This gigantic eel or water serpent lived in the nearby lake and had killed all men and cattle that had gone near. St Patrick said to the man: 'If you lend me your horse, I will enable him, by the power of God I serve, to destroy the *peist*'.

St Patrick then took the horse to a hill overlooking the lake and ordered it to go down and kill the serpent. The horse returned victorious but in the fight it had gone mad so St Patrick, fearing that it would do some harm, ordered it to return to the lake and remain there until the last day.

St Patrick built a church on the hill where he stood to commemorate this great event, and to remind the people of the power of God who rid them of the *peist*. This lake is now known as St Patrick's Lough or Loughpatrick – and the horse is still said to appear in the locality. A stone among the ruins of the old church is said, like many others, to have been marked by St Patrick's knees – the builder of the church.

ST COLMCILLE AND CARRICKMORE

There are many tales and legends connected with St Colmcille and the village of Carrickmore. One such story is that St Colmcille ordered that a bullock should be killed and cooked every night to feed his employees, but he insisted that special care should be taken not to break any of the animal's bones. After the meal the bones were blessed by St Colmcille and placed side by side on a small hill called Mullinalap, adjoining Carrickmore. In the morning the animal could be seen alive and grazing on the top of the hill.

HOW GREENCASTLE OBTAINED ITS NAME

In the days of the *raparee* (highwayman) in Tyrone, a single road ran through this district. One such *raparee* named Frederick collected his 'toll' from wealthy travellers between Derry and Belfast. At a commons beside this road, the ruin of a stone-built cottage had a sod roof with grass. This is where Ellen Ruadh lived, an old woman who was his landlady, and who provided refreshments to the *raparee* when on his rounds. Being a tall man, he once complained ungratefully that her house was too cramped for a man of his size.

Ellen responded: 'It may be small and poor to you, but to me this cottage is my castle!'

'Well, Ellen,' retorted the *raparee*, 'it is indeed a green castle!' and that is allegedly how Greencastle obtained its name.

BESSY BELL HILL

The twin peaks of Bessy Bell and Mary Gray form a gateway to the south of the Sperrins, and it is believed that Bessy Bell Hill (located between Omagh and Newtownstewart) was named by Scottish settlers during the plantation period after a character in an old Scottish folk tale to act as a reminder of home.

CLOGHER'S STONE

According to legend, Clogher took its name from a stone said to have been an altar after the establishment of a Christian church at Clogher; it has been suggested that the Gaelic name of Cloch Óir originated in the exceeding richness of the land which immediately surrounds the town.

FARSNAGH POINT

This area of the western Lough Neagh shoreline is also known as Golloman's Point – and according to legend, while Ardboe Cross was being made, a cow came out of the lough and produced large quantities of milk for the builders. The cow is also reputed to have produced milk that was used to blend the mortar used in the cross. After the work was done, the cow then returned to the lough.

LORD BELMORE'S BENEVOLENCE

In the Dromore area there are many locations of 'Mass Rocks', where Catholics worshipped during the Penal Code era. It is said that Lord Belmore, a local property owner in Dromore, was so impressed with the devotion of the congregation at one such gathering that he made available a piece of ground for the erection of a church. This is where the Catholic church of Dromore now stands.

DEATH CUSTOMS

The wake has been a tradition observed by both Catholics and Protestants across Tyrone. In *Tyrone Folk Quest* by Michael J. Murphy, the customs associated with the wake are described in great detail:

> At the wake house door Francis Henry paused, raised the latch, raised his cap, blessed himself and prayed in silence … women who came in knelt in prayer at the bedside and then joined the company in talk of the dead woman and then on to mundane everyday topics. The men did not kneel in prayer. A plate was passed round containing cigarettes and ready-rubbed plug tobacco.

On the day of a funeral in some parts of Tyrone, salt was carried in mourner's pockets as a protection against evil; also red ribbons were also worn by the men in a funeral procession when the corpse they bore had died a violent death at another's hand.

Another set of wake traditions were known as the 'American' or 'living' wake which marked the departure of people emigrating to another country (see Chapter 5).

SOME TYRONE SUPERSTITIONS

To carry coals from one fire to another in the house was to carry sickness.

One should never look at the back of a haycart on the road or the tail of a white horse without making a wish.

CURES AND CHARMS

There are many customs associated with cures – a recipient might be told not to thank the curer because it would destroy the charm, and many who know the secret of a cure say they cannot reveal it because it would no longer work.

A Cough Cure from County Tyrone

Take a half-pound of honey, 2 ounces of flax seed, two leaves of the mullein plant, one stick of angelica, and one nutmeg. Boil the mullein leaves in a half-pint of new milk until tender. Then set aside to cool. Pour homey over it, then take the flax seeds that have steeped for twenty-four hours and boil them in the water they were steeped in. Strain through muslin, and pour over honey. Boil together briskly, strain and bottle.

A Special Donkey

Pigs weren't the only pet or animal to possess special powers! During past times, there was a special donkey in the Clonoe area. It had the shape of a cross on its back and children suffering from whooping cough were passed under the donkey's belly three times, for three days. For mumps, the donkey's halter was used to lead the sufferer round the well or forge in the hope of affecting a cure.

Donkeys were also used for getting rid of unwanted warts. Bread was rubbed on the wart and then given to a donkey to eat. Another wart cure was to rub it with a penny and leave the penny on the road for a person to lift, while some people thought taking a bag of stones, one for each wart, and leaving it at a nearby crossroads would also work.

People who 'Blinked' Cattle and Horses

According to Frank McVeigh from Dernaseer near Galbally, in his recollections of rural life in South Tyrone in *Our Cornmill and Other Memories*, there were people who 'blinked' cattle and horses. In order that they couldn't be blinked, the farmer would tie a red rag or a bit of cloth on the cow's horn or on the horse's winkers – the leather piece that went over the horse's eyes.

Some people had a charm for the blinking. One woman said that her cow got blinked and she was able to cut a bit of cloth from the person who was accused and burnt it under the cow's head. The sick cow jumped up and was alright after that.

In some old Tyrone houses, the hind-leg bones of a cow might be unearthed in a chimney. They were placed there as a charm against the rest of the cattle getting whatever disease it was that this particular animal had died from.

In Fivemiletown, it was said that if the family cat sat with her back to the fire on the hearth, then it would rain before morning.

Sneezing

Once, people believed that sneezing could banish the soul from the body, so if a person sneezed it was custom to say 'God Bless You'.

Another popular rhyme used in Tyrone (although thought to have originated in England during the nineteenth century) goes:

Sneeze on a Monday, sneeze for danger.
Sneeze on a Tuesday, kiss a stranger.
Sneeze on a Wednesday, get a letter.
Sneeze on a Thursday, maybe better.
Sneeze on a Friday, that's for sorrow.
Sneeze on a Saturday, love comes tomorrow.
Sneeze not on Sunday, but pray.

Miscellaneous Cures

Earache: Roast an onion in the turf ashes and place against ear.
Sore Throat: Stocking filled with hot salt and wrapped about throat.
Heart Disease: Powdered lily of valley root.
Rheumatism: Powdered washing soda in small muslin bag worn over the affected part. Small potato carried in pocket.
Epilepsy: Take and heat a church key, then pass it along the head. It was also considered dangerous to get between an epileptic having a fit and the fire lest the sickness was passed from one to the other.
Deafness: Anoint ear with oil of eels.
Nosebleed: Widow's key at back of the neck.
Toothache: Put a piece of ginger in the tooth.

SACRED PLACES

While St Patrick's Well in the Castlederg area is supposed to have water which is said to help cure the pain of toothache, at one point 'eye wells' were quite common in Ulster. A well-known one stood on the outskirts of Dromore and it was sought for its healing powers from outside the district.

According to local tradition, a farmer once brought his horse who was suffering from an eye infection to the well, for at that time the well was situated beside the road. Shortly after the incident, the well relocated itself several feet from the highway. Another version of this story is that while the horse's eyes improved, the farmer himself went blind.

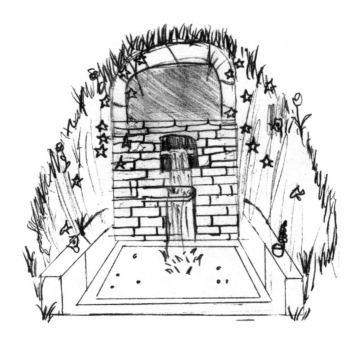

St Patrick's Chair and Well, in Altadevin Glen near Augher

According to folklore, the water within this well – which is said by local people to never run dry – has healing powers; the water from the well is believed to be good at healing warts. Local folklore also maintains that if you sit and make a wish here that within days it will come true.

If a well dried up, then its specific powers were transferred to whatever tree or bush stood nearest to it. One such example is the Pin Tree near Ardboe Cross. This particular tree is supposed to be very lucky and has the power to grant wishes.

It was a 'wishing tree' and was so-called because it had pins and pennies and coins of all kinds, vividly described by Polly Devlin (see Chapter 8) in *The Far Side of the Lough* (The O'Brien Press, 1999):

> brooches and clips and nails, and any odd bits of metal, and most of all with pins; safety pins and sewing pins, any class of pin … everybody believed something about that tree depending on what they wanted to believe … others thought it was a curing tree, that if you left something in it you would get better of your pains. But the belief most people held was that if you put something into the tree you would always come back to fetch it; and that was why metal was always put in, for it lasted the longest.

Lough Neagh

Legend has it that Lough Neagh was created by the Irish giant Finn McCool who scooped out the Lough basin to toss it at a Scottish rival that was fleeing Ulster by way of the Giants Causeway. The piece of land fell into the Irish Channel and formed the Isle of Man.

The 'Washing Bay'

Situated close to Lough Neagh, and located further south of Ardboe, the Washing Bay gets its name from the nearby 'Holy River' which flows into the lough, and which is supposed to have healing powers. In the recorded case of one person whose body was so weak that he could not walk, he bathed in the lough for eight days; his sores dried up, and he grew healthy, married and had children, and lived several years after. Many then frequented the lake who were afflicted with running sores and returned home perfectly healed.

FAIRIES

As in other parts of Ireland, the presence of fairies commands a great deal of consideration and there are many well-known examples of this in Tyrone. It is customary at the Fairy Water (a medium-sized river that rises in the hills above Drumquin) to greet the fairies when passing by the area.

In Clonoe, a local man who returned from Scotland after many years was helping to cut hay in a meadow and decided to cut down a fairy tree. When he hit the tree with the first chop, fire rushed up and singed his face, leaving his eyes bloodshot for the rest of his life. With tales such as this, people were reluctant to cut any fairy trees down as bad luck would befall anyone who did.

A superstition related to fairies was that you could never go outside the house and leave children unless they first set the tongs near the fire. By 'cradling' the tongs, the children were kept safe.

One of Tyrone's most famous poets wrote his own tribute to the 'little people':

> I know a green hill
> Near till a road,
> It's green with the shamrock
> That no man sowed:
> For the shees sowed the shamrock
> An' brought the black bee
> To make it grow forever
> On the steep green lea.

(W.F. Marshall, 'The Fairy Hill')

GHOST STORIES

The White Lady of Seskinore

The village of Seskinore has a legendary tale of the White Lady who is supposed to haunt Cow Lane. The story goes that on the marriage of the only daughter of the owner of the old castle at Mullaghmore to a gallant young sportsman, a hunt was organised as the highlight of the festivities.

Tragically the young man was thrown from his horse and killed at the Fox Covert, now known as Cow Lane. The White Lady of Seskinore, still dressed in her wedding apparel, looks for her husband in Cow Lane.

Davies Bawn

Legend has it that an unfortunate piper is lost forever in a forgotten passageway under the ruins of Davies Bawn in Castlederg. Apparently on still, quiet nights his musical laments can still be heard.

The Black Sergeant

There is a popular tale around the town of Dungannon about the mysterious 'Black Sergeant'. There are many accounts of the sightings of this figure who reportedly stalked the Oaks Road area during the 1950s. Apparently the sergeant was a member of the Royal Irish Constabulary who was shot dead by a colleague in that part of the town many decades before the alleged sightings.

The Stone that Weeps Blood

In Castlecaulfield, it is believed that one of the stones that is an integral part of the castle structure weeps blood. The stone weeps for the long-lost love of a young girl who was imprisoned in the wall of the castle by her father. He would not let her marry a knight in shining armour because he was not considered good enough by the girl's parents. The girl's love died in battle while the girl herself died while imprisoned.

SOME SEASONAL CUSTOMS OF TYRONE

New Year's Day

1 January has been the official start of a New Year since 1751 when the new calendar was established. It was believed that what happened on this date would have a bearing on future events in the year. This was a day for caution, since a mistake made on New Year's Day could be repeated each day throughout the year.

Nothing should be thrown out, not even ashes or tea leaves – for fear of bad luck. On no account should a bill be paid on that day, otherwise you would be handing out money all through the year.

St Brigid's Eve

This fell on 31 January and was traditionally the first day of spring. The tradition of St Brigid's Ribbon was a silk ribbon would be placed outside the house on a window sill on this evening and then kept as a remedy against headaches.

St Brigid's Day

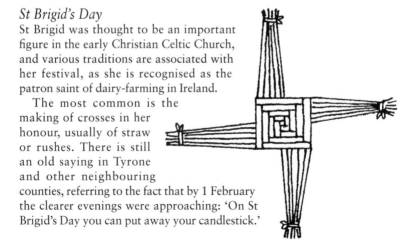

St Brigid was thought to be an important figure in the early Christian Celtic Church, and various traditions are associated with her festival, as she is recognised as the patron saint of dairy-farming in Ireland.

The most common is the making of crosses in her honour, usually of straw or rushes. There is still an old saying in Tyrone and other neighbouring counties, referring to the fact that by 1 February the clearer evenings were approaching: 'On St Brigid's Day you can put away your candlestick.'

St Patrick's Day

The traditional Irish patron saint's feast day was welcomed by many Tyrone people as it was a respite from the strict Lenten fast.

Easter

At Easter, children's hands were rubbed with salt and they were warned not to fall asleep outside in the open air, as the fairies would try and steal them. One source recorded that people knelt to the rising sun and prayed for good health and preservation from sudden death during the year.

Eggs were given as presents and they were decorated and given to children to roll on the hillsides. In some places throughout Tyrone, children made Easter houses of little sticks and boiled eggs over a turf fire.

May Eve

This marked the beginning of summer and people would go out after sunset to gather May flowers. They would take them home and leave a flower at every door about the house for good luck that year.

In Frank McVeigh's recollections, the children would stay up until after midnight to go to the spring well for a can of water. The belief was that whoever was the first at the well at the first day of May would have plenty of milk and butter for that year.

On May Eve, there was also a tradition of fire. Druids lit the 'Bealtaine' fire on the Hill of Uisneach in County Westmeath – and this formed a circle known as the 'inner ring' through other inland counties, which included the summits of hills in Tyrone and in turn prompted people in other counties such as Donegal on the coast to ignite theirs – known as the 'outer ring of fire'.

May Day

In parts of Tyrone it was considered unlucky to be the first house to show smoke on May morning, with the cattle being milked and the byre swept clean before the fire was lit. Two fires were lit and cattle were driven between them as a protection against diseases.

As pigs were considered lucky animals, they were driven into the house on May Day for luck.

One belief was that you shouldn't lend anything on May Day nor throw out ashes, because fairies moved house on 1 May and you would be in trouble if you threw the ashes into their faces.

If you were a visitor on May Day and asked a farmer for milk, a pinch of salt would be added to the pail to prevent the luck of the house being carried away.

The Girl's Fair

Gortin was the venue for a June Fair known as the Girl's Fair, a chance for girls of marriageable age to display themselves to potential suitors. They might prepare themselves for this ordeal with a dish of mutton broth made from the flesh of sheep not good enough for sale.

The Feast of St John

Celebrated on 23 June, this was celebrated by bonfires, when St John's Fire was lit and burned embers taken to every field around to keep away the evil spirits.

Lughnasa

The beginning of harvest fell in August, marking the beginning of the end of the summer. The festival of Lughnasa is named after the sun god Lugh who, legend has it, held funeral games at this time of year for his foster mother Tailtu.

Hallowe'en

This marked the end of the harvest and the onset of winter. It was a time for feasting and merrymaking, games, dares and pranks. In some houses some ashes were left near the grate – and smoothed down to get a footprint mark to see who had visited. Sometimes, the footprints were studied, if they pointed inward there would be a birth in the coming year. If they pointed out, there would be a death.

In recent decades, the custom of children dressing up, wearing masks and collecting coins from homes in their local area became common in Tyrone.

What started off with a recital of a poem or a song soon became the Americanised 'Trick or Treat' which involved the children sometimes playing a trick on the neighbour to get some 'sweets'.

Boxing Day

In parts of Tyrone, the 'Mummers' took to the road and stopped at houses to entertain local folk. The masked tradition of 'Mumming' in Ireland is said to date back 2,500 years. This medieval European folk-drama enacted a death and resurrection theme, particularly at Christmas, the darkest period of the year, with the promise of the return of spring implicit in the return to life of whoever was killed in the fight.

It is a possibility that this is where the term Mummers derives from because the Middle English word *mum* means silent. Thus, Mumming plays began as miming performances. Eventually, words were added, but the original stories have often been partially lost through translation and retellings of the story.

Mumming brings together a number of art forms, including drama, music, poetry and dancing. Groups of men in the guise of colourful characters travelled from house to house – and even local pubs – performing their short rhyming play. While the origins of Mumming and the Mummer's Play aren't definitive, Tyrone had a strong Mummer tradition, which was observed particularly well at Drumquin, Trillick and other areas of West Tyrone.

Generally, Mummer's plays are always in verse and usually the main theme is a combat between two heroes, the fall of one of them, and his revival by a doctor. Following the struggle between the two hero figures, representing the fight between the forces of light and darkness, one falls to the ground. He represents the death of the old year. The doctor has a magic potion which is able to resuscitate the slain character.

While many of the rhymes were brought to Ireland in the sixteenth and seventeenth centuries by the Scottish and English planters, one of the popular Mumming characters in areas of Tyrone is Jack Straw – dressed entirely in straw, his rhyme is occasionally a riddle, and he is followed into combat by Green Knight, dressed in the green colours of Ireland.

God save our shadowed lands
Stalked by this night beast of the dead
– Turnip roundness of the skull,
Sockets smouldering in the head
– will no St George or Patrick come,
Restore to us our once blessed
And blossoming, now barren home?
>   (John Montague, 'The Mummer Speaks', *New Collected Poems*
>   (2012), by kind permission of the author and The Gallery Press)

5

A DIVERSE CULTURE AND SHARED TRADITIONS

The phrase 'cultural traditions' is frequently used when referring to the people and landscape of County Tyrone. There have been two predominant 'traditions' in Tyrone since the plantation, and the reality is that many experiences and themes have been shared, such as place names or symbols like the Red Hand.

With such events as the Flight of the Earls and the Plantation having been marked in recent years with important anniversaries, these were the forerunner to a 'decade of anniversaries'. During this period, events such as the Ulster Solemn League and Covenant, the Easter Rising and Partition will be marked by events that will aim to be inclusive of all memories and experiences relating to sometimes contentious events.

There are also many unique cultural traditions belonging to the nationalist and unionist traditions that are celebrated with great pride in the respective communities.

Some unique traditions and important dates celebrated by the Unionist community include:

THE ORANGE ORDER

At the Battle of the Boyne in 1690, Irish Catholics supported the army of King James II of England and Protestants supported King William of Orange. Following on from the victory of William, the Orange Order was formed at the end of the next century from a number of Protestant organisations which had been in existence. One of these organisations was the Orange Boys, created by James Wilson from Dyan, a small hamlet near Caledon in Tyrone.

The Grand Orange Lodge of Ireland elects its officers annually from the ranks of county lodge officers – there are a total of twelve county lodges in Ireland (including Tyrone) that in turn are drawn from district lodges. Districts are groups of individual local (or private) lodges, and every member must belong to one of these.

1 JULY: SOMME COMMEMORATION

This marks the anniversary of the opening of the Somme campaign in 1916 during the First World War. Many Tyrone people lost their lives during this terrible conflict, and the Orange Order holds church parades and wreath-laying ceremonies on this day and the Sunday nearest to it.

11 JULY: BONFIRE NIGHT

Unionist communities throughout Tyrone have bonfires on the eve of the 'Glorious Twelfth'.

12 JULY: THE GLORIOUS TWELFTH

The Orange Order celebrates the success of King William at the Battle of the Boyne at a number of different venues in Tyrone. Marchers proceed to a field of assembly where religious hymns and prayers are recited. Various towns and villages in Tyrone get the opportunity to host this event once every seven years.

Some unique traditions and important dates celebrated by the Nationalist community include:

THE ANCIENT ORDER OF HIBERNIANS

This Roman Catholic political association was formed in the United States during the 1830s. The chief aims of the association are to work for the independence of Ireland and to promote and preserve the Catholic faith.

The traditional parade day for the Order is 15 August, the Feast of the Assumption. Some will also take part in St Patrick's Day processions. Membership of this organisation expanded greatly during the early decades of the twentieth century with the appointment of Nationalist politician Joe Devlin to the presidency of its ruling body, the Board of Erin.

17 MARCH: ST PATRICK'S DAY

St Patrick's Day is obviously a national celebration in Ireland, but thanks to the patron saints well-documented links to Tyrone there are usually special events to mark his feast day.

The county town of Omagh is always central to this, and in recent years thousands of people have converged on its town centre to enjoy the celebrations, culminating with many colourful floats and costumes in the St Patrick's Day parade.

15 AUGUST: THE FEAST OF THE ASSUMPTION

The Ancient Order of Hibernians organises public parades on special occasions, such as the Feast of the Assumption, which commemorates the death of Mary and her assumption into Heaven. In past times, these parades were accompanied by bands, banners and members wore green-coloured sashes.

LANGUAGES

Apart from the commonly used English language, the use of dialects and languages has had a rich tradition in Tyrone:

The Irish Language – An Teanga Gaeilge
Irish is a Celtic language brought to Ireland by the expansion of the Celts westward across Europe in the first millennium BC. The plantation of English-speakers in the seventeenth century marked the first major contribution to the decline of the language in Tyrone, when the indigenous Irish language was pushed more towards the Sperrins areas of East Tyrone.

One seventeenth-century census estimated there was a total population in Tyrone of 18,330. Of this 8,085 were English or Scots, and 10,245 were Irish. By 1806, it was estimated that approximately 141,000 of the then population of Tyrone spoke Irish (out of a total population of 262,000) – more than half the population.

'Hedge schools', such as the one run by Dr Patrick O'Donnelly (see Chapter 9), were often established in remote areas where danger of detection was least likely to be incurred; they played a vital role in maintaining the Irish language in Tyrone during the penal times.

By 1911, the last year there was an all-Ireland language census, Tyrone had approximately 7,500 Irish speakers; six electoral divisions (including Fallagh, Crockanboy, Glenlark, Mounthamilton, Glenchiel and

Glenroan) actually had more than 30 per cent of their overall population who spoke Irish.

The Gaelic Revival of the late nineteenth century had attracted many Protestants to embrace the language, and an example of this was Alice Milligan. Born at Gortmore, Omagh on 4 September 1866, Alice became a political activist, an organiser for the Gaelic League, and lectured in history throughout Ireland.

She was also a prolific writer, publishing poetry in the *United Irishmen* and helping to edit other journals such as the *Northern Patriot* and the *Shan Van Vocht*. In 1900, she wrote a play, *The Last Feast of the Fianna*, for the Irish Literary Theatre. Her magazines, plays, novels, short stories and poems were published across the world and she had readers in South Africa, America, Europe and South America.

She also founded numerous cultural, literary and feminist organisations from the late nineteenth century on, and travelled the country trying to bring the Irish language and culture to small communities – despite the restrictions of the time.

The latter decades of the twentieth century brought another revival of sorts of *An Ghaeilge*. Irish speaking is currently thriving in Tyrone and this has been greatly helped by the introduction of Irish medium education at nursery, primary and secondary school level in various towns and villages across the county.

The availability of Irish classes to adult learners at local level has also proved popular in recent years, with one such example being *Pobal Mhuileann an tSiáin*: a community group based in Sion Mills who organise weekly Irish Language classes and have also developed the online learning resource www.easyirish.com.

Some phrases/questions in Irish:

Fáilte go contae Thír Eoghain – Welcome to County Tyrone

Caisleáin agus croiche – Castles and crosses

Tír Eoghain abú – Up Tyrone (popular in a Gaelic games context)

Dearg agus Bán – Red and white (the Tyrone GAA colours)

Ulster Scots – Ullans

Ulster Scots, or Ullans, is spoken by about 35,000 people in the north of Ireland. It is a regional variation of Scots, a language still spoken in the Lowlands of Scotland which shares its roots with standard English but was subject to a different development over the centuries. The dialect is regarded as a language by many and was brought to the north of Ireland during the Ulster Plantation.

The term Ulster-Scots has, for nearly 400 years, referred to people, not place – the people who migrated from Scotland to Ulster – and to the Ulster-Scots communities that they established right across the province.

The Ulster variant of Scots developed most strongly in those areas where the planters settled in concentrated numbers such as Antrim and East Down and East Donegal – and it is in these areas that most speakers of Ulster-Scots can be found today.

However, Tyrone also has a proud Ulster-Scots speaking heritage, and many distinguished writers and linguists have come from the Ulster-Scots tradition in Tyrone, such as W.F. Marshall and John Dunlap.

Two watershed events have been the founding of the Ulster-Scots Language Society in 1992 to encourage greater awareness of the dialect/ language, and the establishment of the Ulster-Scots Agency in 1999 as part of the new cross-border language body created under the Good Friday Agreement.

The Agreement of April 1998 was the first official document to mention Ulster-Scots, stating in part that:

> All participants recognize the importance of respect, understanding and tolerance in relation to linguistic diversity, including in Northern Ireland, the Irish language, Ulster-Scots and the languages of the various ethnic communities, all of which are part of the cultural wealth of the island of Ireland ...

Although treated by many linguists as a dialect of English, it has many popular words and phrases:

A quare gunk – a big surprise
Clishmaclaver – idle talk or gossip
Furnenst – opposite, facing
Kep tha banes green – keep healthy
Yestreen – last night

SHARED TRADITIONS

Emigration

Perhaps the greatest shared tradition in County Tyrone is that of emigration, and it is a major theme that has affected members of every religious denomination of every town and village in the county. Whilst internal migration within Ireland has always been one option for Tyrone people – William Carleton (see Chapter 8) is a fine example of this, as he arrived in Dublin by foot from his native Clogher Valley in 1818, – the opportunity to travel and settle in other continents has been taken by thousands of Tyrone people.

'The desire to emigrate is no fundamental part of the natural make-up of man' according to historian R.J. Dickson. It was economic necessity that led thousands of people away from their natural home to find better opportunities in North America, and later, Britain, Australia and other places around the world.

The Penal Laws intended to outlaw the Catholic faith; however, Presbyterians were also 'circumscribed' and were debarred from holding office under the Crown. They were also debarred from owning freehold land; they could only obtain leases, with rents that increased on renewal.

They often had no emotional attachment to land they could not own, so in their thousands they sold their leases and their stock and set sail for North America where they could worship as they wanted, and buy land cheaply.

Among the most famous Tyrone emigrants were the Mellon family, who amassed great fortunes in the New World, and later became prime benefactors for the creation of the Ulster American Folk Park. Indeed, Protestants formed the majority of the emigrants to North America in the eighteenth century, one example being John Dunlap – the printer of the first copies of the Declaration of Independence in the United States.

During the nineteenth century it became more common for Roman Catholics to seek better economic conditions in the New World. One such example was James Shields, who became a United States senator.

The American Wake

For many of those emigrants who departed from Tyrone in the eighteenth and nineteenth centuries, the hours before departure became known as the 'American' or 'Living' Wake. Departure was a kind of death, especially when a voyage across the ocean to America could last months and the prospect of a return was fairly remote.

At these wakes, friends and family shared one last time with those whom they would probably never in life see again. It usually began at night time, in the house of the emigrant, and continued through the night until the early hours.

In some areas, the American Wake proved to be a festive occasion. Neighbours frequently brought food. While the men sat talking in subdued tones, drinking *uisce beatha* (whiskey – the 'water of life'), the wife or mother of the emigrant was exempt from duties in deference to her grief. The sorrow of those left behind was equally acute for those leaving.

The Emigrants' Experience

Tyrone emigrant James Murray found America more than satisfactory thanks to a combination of economic and political freedom it offered. In 1737, he took the time to write a letter home to his Presbyterian minister so that he might mention his experience to family and friends:

Read this letter, and look, and tell aw [all] the poor folk of your place, that god has opened a door for their deliverance; for here is ne [no] scant of bread … Ye may get Lan (land) here for 10 pund a hundred acres for ever, and ten years tell ye get the money before they wull ask ye for it …

Desire my fether and mether too, and my three sisters to come here … and I will pay their passage … this York is as big as twa [two] of Armagh … There is servants comes here out of Ereland, and have served there [*sic*] time here, wha [who] are now Justices of the Piece [*sic*].

This letter was typical of thousands that brought news of prosperity in places such as New York in the American colonies to homes in Tyrone and other parts of Ireland. However, it wasn't a pleasant experience for every emigrant.

Over 100 years later, on a summer's night in 1855, Thomas McIntyre, a house-plasterer from County Tyrone sat down in his boarding house in Boston. Weary and sore from his day's labour, he wrote a letter to his sister back home in the village of Donemana that illustrated the loneliness felt by many emigrants, here is an extract:

August 27, 1855
Dear Sister,
I know today you are all, or at least a good part of you, at Donemana Fair. I am just thinking as I sit here alone of the times I used to have on these occasions. But there are no Donemana Fairs here. There is nothing here but work hard today and go to bed at night and rise and work harder tomorrow … Give my love to all my old neighbours and friends. You will scarce be able to make this handwriting out – I was just beginning to think that I had the trowel in my hand.
Farewell all,
T. McIntyre
Write soon.

The Ulster-American Folk Park

One of the main tourist attractions located in Tyrone that appeals to international visitors is the Ulster-American Folk Park. The park is an indoor and outdoor museum that is built around the theme of emigration in the eighteenth and nineteenth centuries.

Situated at Camphill, just a few miles north of Omagh, the Folk Park initially began by the donation of a cottage by the Mellon family. Their original farmstead was restored and opened to the public in 1968 and it was around this that the Folk Park evolved.

This ancestral home of Thomas Mellon depicts the rural lifestyle of the times and the New World to which he emigrated in 1818; his parents set up home in Westmoreland County, Pennsylvania after selling their 23-acre farm for 200 guineas – a small fortune at that time. Thomas Mellon went on to become a judge, banker and millionaire.

One of his sons, Andrew, became secretary to the United States Treasury, and was the man responsible for building many large companies such as Gulf Oil and US Steel. In 1937, he donated his entire art collection, worth more than $35 million, to the federal government, which established the National Gallery of Art in Washington DC.

The Ulster-American Folk Park also includes the rebuilt childhood home of Archbishop John Hughes, the first Catholic Archbishop of New York, moved from its original site in County Monaghan.

Archbishop John Hughes

The Tyrone-born cleric became Archbishop of New York on 19 July 1850. One of the most influential Irish Americans of his time, he was dispatched by Abraham Lincoln as an envoy to Europe at a critical juncture of the American Civil War.

He was born in Annaloughan, a townland in the parish of Clogher but several years later his family moved to another farm nearby in the townland of Dernaved, County Monaghan. It was from this farmhouse that John, as a young man of 20, departed for America in 1817, where his family had settled in Chambersburg, Pennsylvania.

The transition of the Tyrone/Irish emigrant to America is carefully recorded and the visitor can travel between Old and New World via a transitional ship, before stepping into a replica Pennsylvania village from the nineteenth century.

Among the key outdoor exhibits is a reconstructed Pennsylvania farm that is a faithful replica of the Mellon farmstead in the United States, with its attendant Log Barn, Smoke House, Corn Crib and Spring House. There is also a blacksmith's forge and a schoolhouse in the style of the nineteenth century.

The Folk Park's activities include exhibitions and tours. It celebrates all the North American festivals, especially American Independence Day on 4 July, and has a Bluegrass music festival during the late summer months.

The Centre for Migration Studies is also situated close to the main entrance of the Folk Park; this is an excellent resource centre for those interested in finding out information about their family history.

Links between Tyrone and North America

Towns and villages named Tyrone in the United States and Canada:

Tyrone (Georgia) founded 1911
Tyrone (New York) founded 1822
Tyrone (Ontario) founded *circa* 1830
Tyrone (Pennsylvania) founded 1850

There are also 'county communities' named Tyrone in the states of Colorado, Kentucky, Missouri and West Virginia, while Tyrone in New Mexico has been a 'ghost town' for almost a century!

There are also many towns throughout North America named after Tyrone towns and villages; for example, Stewartstown in Pennsylvania and Dungannon in Virginia.

Tyrone's link to the American Presidents

Tyrone has a proud link to at least three American presidents: James Buchanan, the 15th President; Ulysses Simpson Grant, the 18th President; and Woodrow Wilson, the 28th President.

James Buchanan

The father of President Buchanan (1857–61) emigrated from the ancestral home at Deroran near Omagh, and the president was born in a log cabin in Franklin County, Pennsylvania in 1791.

Woodrow Wilson

President Wilson's ancestral home is based at Dergalt, near Strabane. This dwelling was built in the late eighteenth century and is the homestead of his grandfather, James Wilson. It is a traditional one-room wide cottage, and is situated on the scenic Plumbridge to Strabane road. The house is furnished as it was in the early nineteenth century, the main room was the kitchen, and the point around which the life of the house revolved was the open turf fire.

Ulysses Simpson Grant

The 18th President of the United States had distinctly Tyrone roots – and was the first President of the United States to visit Ireland. Ulysses Simpson Grant held office from 1869 to 1877, but he had already achieved much recognition as being the leading Union general in the American Civil War.

On 27 April 1822, Grant was born in a log cabin in Point Pleasant, Clermont County, Ohio. He was the eldest of the six children of Jesse Root Grant (1794–1873) and Hannah Simpson Grant (1798–1883). Hannah's father was John Simpson who was born in County Tyrone, at Dergnagh (in Irish, 'red, marshy ground'), between Dungannon and Ballygawley, in 1738. He migrated to Pennsylvania aged 22 in 1760.

John Simpson's grandson reached prominence by taking Fort Henry in 1862 – one of the first Union victories of the American Civil War. Having ventured into politics following his successful army career, Grant was elected President of the United States as a Republican in 1868. He was the first President to serve for two full terms since Andrew Jackson forty years before.

Ulysses Grant's five-day tour throughout Ireland in 1879 was part of a world tour after his two-term presidency ended – and led him by rail from Dublin through Louth, and then in a circuit throughout Ulster for overnight stays in Derry and Belfast. He also found time to visit his paternal great-grandfather's home in Tyrone.

There have been subsequent reminders of the ex-president in Ireland. In 1907, the immense steamship christened the *President Grant* was built at the Belfast shipyard he had visited; and the Grant Ancestral Homestead near Dungannon, in County Tyrone's Clogher Valley has been restored in recent decades, offering tourists a glimpse of Grant's Irish ties as well as nineteenth-century life in rural Ireland.

The cottage came into public ownership in the 1970s. During restoration, it was discovered that there were large sections of mud walls reinforced with reeds, and an original mud and wattle canopy fireplace came to light, immediately dating the homestead to the fifteenth century. Today the homestead and farm have been restored to the style and appearance of the mid-eighteenth-century small holding.

MARKETS AND HIRING FAIRS

Apart from emigration, another theme that had a major social impact on people in Tyrone was the markets and hiring fairs. In the nineteenth century, these continued to provide trade and entertainment for ordinary people. They were held in almost every town and village in Tyrone, and throughout the province of Ulster.

The weekly market in each location usually sold linen and other popular items such as corn and potatoes. Farm animals such as pigs, horses and sheep were also sold in places such as Fintona, Moy and Stewartstown.

Moy was particularly noted for its horse fair, as horses were in great demand by the cavalry and artillery regiments of the British Army up to and during the First World War. One interesting feature of the Moy Fair was that buyers and horse traders came from all over Europe to attend.

MOY WEEKLY MARKET

WILL OPEN ON

SATURDAY, Nov. 1st, 1879,

And each succeeding SATURDAY, at the hour of TEN o'clock a.m., for the Sale and Purchase of

Pork, Butter, Eggs, Fowl, Pigs, Grain, Potatoes, Hay, Straw, Turnips, &c. &c.

CHEAP TRANSIT OF GOODS

Cheap Inland and Through Rates to all parts of the United Kingdom, for all descriptions of Produce Sold in Moy Market, have been procured direct from Trew and Moy Railway Station.

Buyers have also the choice of facilities of cheap and ready Transit to Belfast and Newry from the Quay, 150 yards distant from the Market Place, by Blackwater River, Lough Neagh, Belfast Canal, Bann River and Newry Canal; giving advantages to MOY far above those of any Inland Market Town in Ireland.

BANKING

A Bank Branch has been established for the convenience of those who transact business in the Market.

MARKET ACCOMMODATION

Buyers and Sellers will have, Free of Cost, for the protection of their property, from rain or unfavorable weather, Slated Sheds covering 500 square yards of space; and for their convenience and accommodation the ample room afforded by the enclosed Market Place and Square of the Town of Moy.

Buyers and Sellers may rely on the active help of the Committee and people of the Town.

JUSTICE IN WEIGHING

Beams of the most expensive and perfect kind have been procured, and the strictest care will be taken with regard to Scales, Weights, and Weighing, so that equal justice may be done to Buyers and Sellers. Constant supervision will be exercised, and Police Inspection carefully maintained.

TELEGRAPHIC AND POSTAL

Moy is a head Post Office having Money Order, Savings' Bank and Telegraph Departments complete, thus affording every facility and instant communication with all the great Home and Foreign Markets.

Arrangements are being made for cheap and efficient Cartage from the Market to the Railway.

Moy, October 11th, 1879.   (BY ORDER OF THE COMMITTEE.)

A. RICHARDSON, MACHINE PRINTER, BOOKP... ... &c, CHURCH STREET, DUNGANNON.

Hiring also took place and Tyrone was a county that was strongly associated with this practice. Prospective employees offered themselves for work on farms and household duties to farmers for the agricultural season. Towns and villages such as Strabane, Cookstown, Ballygawley and Aughnacloy were among the most popular centres.

Labourers' wages in the nineteenth century were considered small at tenpence a day in winter and a shilling in summer. By the outbreak of the First World War, hired men were earning £10 and women £6 a half-year together with their food and lodging.

The younger hirees were usually accompanied by their parents – and it was they who did the bargaining with the farmer. Their treatment varied from farm to farm, and when the annual contract expired, the fair was the meeting place for those who had left home for such employment. There was great entertainment at these fairs, with ballads and variety acts among the many attractions.

In Dungannon, those wanting work used to assemble at the corner of Market Square where Scotch Street meets Irish Street until someone came to offer them work, but hiring in this way is believed to have died out in Dungannon by the mid-1930s.

Neighbouring Cookstown had a weekly market and twice-yearly fair that dated back to 1628 and took place on 12 May and 13 November; if these dates didn't fall on a Saturday, it was held on the Saturday (Cookstown market day) prior to them.

It took place anywhere along the main street from the Fair Hill or Loy Street to Oldtown. The sale of turf was a speciality in Cookstown, and while outlying villages and hamlets such as Orritor had their own fairs they declined as those in Cookstown became much more successful.

It was Strabane, however, that hosted the biggest hiring fair in Tyrone. As in most towns, the main fairs each lasted two days and were held in May and November. Strabane's fairs served not only the immediate area but a wider hinterland stretching from West Donegal to Cavan and Monaghan. The last one took place on 12 May 1949.

At Strabane, before the First World War, the annual wages were as follows:

£12 for a ploughman
£9 for a strong female servant
£5 for a young boy or girl, living with the family household.

Some Tyrone fairs dated back as far as the seventeenth century, including those at Trillick, Killeter and Drumquin. Many of the people who were hired came from the west coast of Donegal, including Patrick 'the Cope' Gallagher who later became famous for his shops in Donegal.

> Attention pay, you country folk, a wee while if you please,
> I'll sing to you a verse or two, to amuse you at my ease.
> It's all about a handsome girl, her equal would be rare,
> And the first place that I met her was in Killeter Fair.
>
> Chorus:
> Her eyes they shone like diamonds, and her cheeks bloomed like the rose,
> She is my first, my only love, no matter where she goes.

> She stole my heart completely, boys, the truth I must declare,
> And the first place that I met her was in Killeter Fair.
>> (Francis Kelly, 'The Old Ballad of Killeter Fair')

The hiring fairs were in decline by the 1930s. Among the reasons for this were that workers sought better work, better conditions and better wages in England and Scotland; while the introduction of compulsory school attendance cut off young labour, and the introduction of limited social welfare payments decreased the supply of older servants.

PRESERVING CULTURAL TRADITIONS IN A LOCAL CONTEXT IN TYRONE

There are many community organisations who have recognised the value in preserving artefacts and other items that relate to valuable cultural traditions. One example of this important practice in Tyrone is the Nally Heritage Centre at Carrickmore St Colmcille's Gaelic Football Club.

This centre opened on 22 March 2009 and is named after Patrick William Nally, one of the founders of the Gaelic Athletic Association. The link with this historical figure is that the Carrickmore club is now custodian of the 'Nally Stand' from Croke Park in Dublin.

The centre is inclusive of social, economic, political and sporting history relating to the local area. There are several exhibits including 'Social Life of the People' which examines the impact of churches, education and housing evolution on the lives of the people from as early as the fifth century. Another display focuses on the 'Townlands of Termonmaguirk' which gives an overview of the geographical history of the parish and how it evolved to hold its current boundaries.

THE 'NEWCOMER'

In recent decades, Tyrone has become a much more cosmopolitan place, with a rapidly changing environment by virtue of an influx of 'newcomer' migrants. Today in Tyrone there are individuals, families and communities from many countries across the world, such as Poland, Latvia, Lithuania, East Timor and Portugal. Dungannon is one area that has experienced very high proportions of migrants from European Union (7.8 per cent) and Non-EU (2.6 per cent) countries compared to the overall figures for Northern Ireland (2.5 per cent and 2.0 per cent respectively).

6

NOTABLE TYRONE PEOPLE AND THEIR IMPACT

A plethora of Tyrone people have achieved great success in their chosen careers – and in many cases, they have made an impact on a global scale. Tyrone emigrants and their descendants have reached the lofty position of Presidents and Governors of other countries among other positions of responsibility and prestige.

This is just a small selection of notable Tyrone people, a sample from various parts of the county who have achieved some notable success during their lifetime, either at home in Tyrone or elsewhere in the world and, in some cases, both.

The Ulster History Circle is a small, not-for-profit organisation that places commemorative blue plaques in public places across Ulster, including villages and towns in County Tyrone. This honours men and women who have contributed in their own way to the history of Tyrone. The Ulster History Circle was formed in the 1980s to acknowledge the achievements of various people from the province of Ulster. Five of the following seven people have been honoured by the Ulster History Circle with a plaque.

JOHN KING: ONE OF THE FIRST PEOPLE TO CROSS AUSTRALIA

He may be a relatively unknown historical figure in Tyrone, but in Australia John King is still revered as a legend, more than 140 years after his death. He was a member of the famous Burke and Wills expedition across Australia, of which he was the sole survivor.

The expedition was organised by the Royal Society of Victoria; its aim was to become the first to cross the continent of Australia from Melbourne on the south coast to the Gulf of Carpentaria on the north coast.

Those involved in the expedition travelled around 3,000 miles from Melbourne to the shores of the Gulf of Carpentaria and then back to the

Depot Camp at Cooper Creek. Seven men died in the attempt, including the leader, Robert O'Hara Burke, and the third in command, William John Wills.

John King was born in Moy on 15 December 1838 to Henry and Ellen King, and was the youngest of four siblings. John was educated at the Royal Hibernian Military School at Phoenix Park in Dublin, before joining the 70th Regiment in January 1853. He was sent to Chatham and was later stationed in Peshawar in the North West Frontier Province of India where he was involved in some of the principal engagements during the Indian Mutiny.

While convalescing from a severe illness, he met George Landells, who had been sent to India by the Victorian Government in Australia to purchase twenty-four camels to be used for exploration of the Australian desert. King was attracted to this different type of adventure and obtained his army discharge in Rawalpindi in January 1860, before arriving in Melbourne on 8 June of that year. His only sister, Elizabeth, had migrated before her younger brother to Australia in 1858.

Robert O'Hara Burke was appointed leader of the Victorian Exploring Expedition, as it was formally known, while William John Wills was surveyor and astronomical observer. John King was appointed as one of the expedition assistants and was placed in charge of the camels.

The expedition departed from Melbourne on 20 August 1860 with a total of eighteen men, twenty-five camels and twenty-two horses. Burke split the expedition at Menindee and the lead party reached Cooper Creek on the border of Queensland and South Australia on 11 November 1860 where they formed a depot. The remaining men were expected to follow up from Menindee and so after a break, Burke decided to proceed to the Gulf of Carpentaria.

Burke split the party again and left on 16 December 1860, placing William Brahe in charge of the depot on Cooper Creek. Burke, Wills, King and Charley Gray reached the estuary of the Flinders river, near where the town of Normanton now stands, on 9 February 1861. They had reached their intended destination.

The men's return trip was disastrous to say the least. Already weakened by starvation and exposure, progress on the return journey was slow and hampered by tropical monsoon downpours.

Charley Gray died on the morning of Wednesday 17th April 1861; but Burke, Wills and King attempted to reach the ominously named Mount Hopeless, the furthest extent of settlement in South Australia, which was closer than Menindee. However, they failed and returned to Cooper Creek.

While waiting for rescue, Burke and Wills died of exhaustion and starvation. King survived with the help of Aborigines until he was rescued a few months later, in September 1861, by Alfred William Howitt. When Howitt reached Menindee he sent King on ahead to Melbourne, escorted by Edwin Welch and Weston Phillips. They arrived in Melbourne on

---

DID YOU KNOW?

To mark the notable anniversary of 150 years since the Burke-Wills expedition departed from Melbourne, the Dungannon & South Tyrone Borough Council, together with the O'Neill Country Historical Society, organised an exhibition in the village of Moy, where John King was born and raised. Launched on 23 August 2010, the event was attended by the Australian Ambassador to Ireland.

---

29 November 1861, and the Irish explorer received a hero's welcome, with flags and bunting on display.

Poignantly, he was present at the inauguration of the Burke & Wills statue on the corner of Collins and Russell Streets in Melbourne on 21 April 1865, the fourth anniversary of their return to Cooper Creek. His popularity also resulted in several newly mapped features – for instance King's Canyon and King's Creek – being named after him.

Later that year, King bought a house in Octavia Street, St Kilda, and on 22 August 1871 he married Mary Richmond. He never fully recovered from the exertions suffered while on the expedition, and by 1869 his health began to deteriorate.

John King died of pulmonary tuberculosis on 15 January 1872 and is buried in the Quaker section of Melbourne General Cemetery, a short distance from Burke and Wills. Thanks to his achievement in becoming the first person to cross the Australian continent, his place is assured in his adopted home.

JAMES MACCULLAGH: MATHEMATICIAN AND PHYSICIST (PLUMBRIDGE)

The eldest of twelve children, James MacCullagh was born in the townland of Landahussy in the parish of Upper Badoney in 1809. He was to become one of Ireland and Europe's most prominent mathematicians and physicists but, like any genius, he had his flaws. In his case this was a deep self questioning insecurity together with a powerful urge towards achievement.

He entered Trinity College Dublin aged just 15 years and took a fellowship in 1832. He was accepted as a member of the Royal Irish Academy the following year before attaining the position of Chair of Mathematics in 1835. He held this position until 1843 and subsequently became Professor of Natural and Experimental Philosophy from 1843 to

> **DID YOU KNOW?**
>
> *Although not a wealthy man, James MacCullagh purchased the early twelfth-century Cross of Cong from the parish priest of Cong, County Mayo, using what was at that time his life savings. On presenting it to the Irish Academy, he stated that his motivation for acquiring it was 'to save it from the shameful process of destruction to which everything venerable in Ireland has been exposed for centuries and to contribute at the same time, to the formation of a national collection'.*

1847. He introduced studies of electricity, heat and terrestrial magnetism into the fellowship course.

MacCullagh won many awards and received great recognition during his own lifetime, including being awarded the Copley Medal for his work 'On surfaces of the second order' in 1842. He devoted much of the remainder of his life to the work of the Royal Irish Academy, but his interests went beyond mathematical physics. He played a key role in building up the academy's collection of Irish antiquities, now housed in the National Museum of Ireland.

In August 1847 he stood unsuccessfully as a parliamentary candidate for one of the Dublin University seats. His failure to win the Dublin University seat for the Liberals, possibly combined with the stress associated with an intense workload, contributed to his tragic death on 24 October 1847.

The following week, on Monday 1 November, much of Dublin came to a standstill as the remains of Professor MacCullagh made their way through the city. Having reached the top of Rutland Street, the procession halted as his body was removed to the hearse, which was to convey the corpse to Tyrone. His last resting place is in the MacCullagh family vault at St Patrick's Church, Upper Badoney.

MARGARET NOBLE: WRITER AND INDIAN NATIONALIST (DUNGANNON)

Tyrone native Margaret Noble led a remarkable life full of achievements – but was perhaps best known as an educationalist and supporter of Indian nationalism in her important role as 'Sister Nivedita'. She was born on 28 October 1867, at Scotch Street in Dungannon, County Tyrone; the eldest of the three surviving children of Samuel Richmond Noble, and his wife, Mary Isabella, *née* Hamilton.

Samuel Noble abandoned the life of a draper to train for religious ministry in Manchester while Margaret remained in Ireland with her grandmother. Margaret was reunited with her parents, who by then had a second daughter, May, when her father was attached to his first church in Oldham.

Following their father's death, Margaret and May were sent to the Congregationalist College at Halifax. In 1884 Margaret took up her first teaching post in Keswick in the Lake District of England, and after a short time she moved to Rugby where she taught in an orphanage.

Her subsequent work at a school in the mining town of Wrexham intensified her interest in social issues, which is said to have stemmed from her father's pastoral work, and had really helped to shape her attitude to those less fortunate than herself.

The death in Wrexham of an intended husband led Margaret to move to Chester, and so closer to Liverpool where her family had resettled. It also triggered a phase of religious scepticism and wider study of different religions. She was influenced by the teaching methods of Friedrich Froebel among others, and became co-founder of a progressive school in Wimbledon which put these principles into action, in 1890.

In 1893, as a member of the London Sesame Club (originally a progressive educational society), she spoke in favour of the second Home Rule Bill. It was there that she heard a Hindu thinker named Swami Vivekananda in London in 1895 and joined his Ramakrishna Order.

His principles and teachings prompted and inspired her to do something for the welfare of the women of India. Margaret began practicing meditation, and sought to lead a very simplistic life. In 1897 she was invited to India, and became Sister Nivedita (meaning 'the dedicated'). She tried to establish a school in Calcutta, but was initially unsuccessful.

Nivedita also assisted in relief work organised by the Ramakrishna Order and began to write and lecture in praise of Hindu culture. Among her publications is *The Web of Indian Life*, which is regarded in India as a good account of Hindu society written in English.

In 1900 Nivedita returned to England with Vivekananda, partly to raise money to relaunch her school. Within months of Nivedita's return to India in 1902, Vivekananda died and Nivedita publicly severed her

---

DID YOU KNOW?

Margaret Noble's extensive publications, lectures, and correspondence were later published in The Complete Works of Sister Nivedita *and* Letters of Sister Nivedita *(both 1982).*

connection with the Ramakrishna Order to commit herself to 'nation building'.

She was in favour of Indian nationalism and lobbied British Members of Parliament to try and influence their thinking on the issue. Having defended British rule on her arrival in India, Nivedita declared in 1901 that India must 'turn them out', and she was one of the first to propose a design for an Indian national flag in 1904. She also collected Indian myths and stories.

Her primary aim was to bring about an improvement in the lives of Indian women belonging to various social classes and castes, and valiantly attempted to bridge the gap and put an end to the infamous caste distinctions. She had good relations with many intellectuals of the Bengali community such as Rabindranath Tagore, the famous Nobel laureate writer – who called her 'a mother of the people'.

Sister Nivedita's health deteriorated after she contracted malaria in 1905, and when she died on 13 October 1911, her body was cremated in Darjeeling, and a memorial to her is inscribed: 'Here reposes Sister Nivedita, who gave her all to India.'

Her life is remembered and indeed celebrated in her native Ireland as well as her adopted India: a commemorative postage stamp was issued in India to mark the centenary of her birth. By the early 1990s an image of Sister Nivedita had been installed in the Matri (Mothers') shrine in the Bharat Mata temple at Hardwar, dedicated to Mother India. Here in Ireland, her life and works were acknowledged with a 'blue plaque' unveiled by the Ulster History Circle at Scotch Street Dungannon in December 2007.

JOE SHERIDAN: INVENTOR OF IRISH COFFEE

Born in Bridgetown, near Castlederg in 1909, Joe Sheridan was one of seven children of Michael and Mary Margaret Sheridan. In 1928, the family moved to Dublin. Joe was working there when he successfully applied for the position of chef at the new restaurant in Foynes terminal building, County Limerick, during 1943.

As a chef, he catered for passengers of the early trans-Atlantic flights who were jet-lagged and weary from their long and sometimes traumatic journeys. Late one night in the winter of 1943, a flight departed Foynes for Botwood, Newfoundland. After flying for several hours in bad weather, the captain made the decision to return to Foynes and await better conditions. A Morse code message was sent to the control tower at Foynes to inform them of their return.

Staff were contacted to return to work and when the flight landed they were brought to the airport restaurant for food and drink to warm them. When Joe was asked to prepare something warm for the passengers, he decided to put some Irish whiskey into their coffees. One of the passengers approached the chef and thanked him for the wonderful coffee.

He asked Joe if he use Brazilian coffee. Joe jokingly answered, 'No, that was Irish coffee!' His idea to make a coffee drink with a distinct twist of Irish whiskey became an instant success. It wasn't long before the story of Irish coffee spread throughout America. One place where it was popularised was in San Francisco, and that was largely thanks to Stanton Delaplane, a travel writer who is credited with introducing it to the Buena Vista Hotel.

In October 1945, as the era of the flying boat came to an end, Foynes Airbase closed in order to make way for landplanes. A new airport was opened on the other side of the Shannon Estuary – Rineanna, which is now known as Shannon International Airport.

Joe Sheridan took his famous drink to the new airport and then, in 1952, he was offered the opportunity to spread his wings. He accepted a position at the Buena Vista in San Francisco where he continued to make and introduce customers to his uniquely Irish creation. A memorial plaque at his graveside in Oakland, California, is inscribed with the words, 'Here lies Joe Sheridan, the inventor of the world's most famous drink: Irish Coffee.'

Joe Sheridan's original idea was celebrated in 2013 to mark its seventieth anniversary with a three-day festival that featured the Irish

---

DID YOU KNOW?

Joe Sheridan's original recipe for Irish coffee is a combination of four key ingredients:

Cream – Rich as an Irish Brogue
Coffee – Strong as a Friendly Hand
Sugar – Sweet as the Tongue of a Rogue
Whiskey – Smooth as the Wit of the Land

Method:
Heat a stemmed whiskey goblet. Pour in one jigger of Irish whiskey. Add one spoon of brown sugar. Fill with strong black coffee to within one inch of the brim. Stir to dissolve the sugar. Top off with whipped cream, slightly aerated, by pouring it over the back of a spoon, so that it floats. Do not stir after adding the cream as the true flavour is obtained by drinking the hot coffee and Irish whiskey through the cream.

coffee-making championship. As for the drink itself, it continues to be served in the original terminal building at Foynes Flying Boat Museum – and also to all dignitaries arriving at Shannon Airport.

DR GEORGE SIGERSON: POET, SCHOLAR AND SENATOR

The term 'man of many talents' is appropriate to describe Dr George Sigerson, who accomplished a great deal during the course of his life. Born on 11 January 1836 at Holy Hill near Strabane, Dr Sigerson was widely known throughout Ireland as an authority on medicine and a writer on scientific subjects.

He was an outstanding linguist and developed a keen interest in poetry, folklore and song, gaining a distinguished reputation as a translator of Gaelic poetry.

His early education in Strabane and Letterkenny Academy prepared him for college life in France, before returning to university life in Galway, Cork and Dublin, from where he graduated in medicine.

Dr Sigerson was appointed Examiner in Natural Science (1862), Fellow (1884) by the Catholic University and Professor of Botany, later Zoology by University College Dublin (UCD) where he lectured from 1908–1923.

Some of Sigerson's works included translations from French into English and from Irish into English, with his book *The Poets and Poetry of Munster* (1860) providing the groundwork for his later work, *Bards of the Gael and Gall*, published in 1897. He occasionally wrote about Tyrone. The famous ballad 'The Mountains of Pomeroy' was penned as a tribute to an area of his native county.

Dr Sigerson taught himself Irish and was a major figure in the Irish Literary Revival in the late nineteenth and early twentieth centuries. His home at Clare Street, Dublin, was a popular meeting place for aspiring Irish writers, poets and musicians.

His reputation as a patriot and scholar was cemented with his donation in 1911 of the renowned university's Gaelic football trophy – the Sigerson Cup – from his own UCD salary, for annual competition among third-level colleges. Sigerson's last book, *The Easter Song of Sedulius*, was published when he was 86. He served as President of the Free State Senate for a period from 1922–23. Dr Sigerson died in 1925 and is buried in Glasnevin Cemetery in Dublin.

DID YOU KNOW?

The Sigerson Cup is modelled on an ancient drinking vessel – The Mether – which is symbolic to friendship, and the four handles of the trophy represent each of the four Irish provinces.

JOHN DUNLAP: SOLDIER AND PRINTER OF THE DECLARATION OF AMERICAN INDEPENDENCE

John Dunlap was born in Meetinghouse Street, Strabane in the year 1747. The family home was described as a large thatched house with a small garden at the rear which ran down steeply to the banks of the river. The actual building was demolished in 1895 to make way for a terrace of three houses. The site is marked by a plaque erected by Strabane Council in 1965 which was unveiled by the then Prime Minister of Northern Ireland, Captain Terence O'Neill.

When he was 10 years old, John went to work as an apprentice to his uncle, William Dunlap, a leading printer and bookseller in Philadelphia, Pennsylvania. In 1766, his uncle sold his stock of books and put his printing house in the care of his nephew in order to pursue religious ministry.

Two years later, William Dunlap became rector of a parish in Virginia, and surrendered his shop and equipment to his nephew. Dr Benjamin Rush, a close friend, reported that John was so poor at first that he lived in his shop, sleeping on the floor under his counter.

Initially John made a living by printing and selling books, but within a few years had switched the emphasis to printing and selling newspapers. It was a shrewd decision at a time of growing political tension in the colonies, where there was an increasing appetite for news.

In November 1771, Dunlap began the publication of the weekly *Pennsylvania Packet and General Advertiser* newspaper – one which supported the rights of the colonies. It was as editor of this newspaper that he wrote home to encourage more of his fellow Irishmen to emigrate to America:

> The young men of Ireland who wish to be free and happy should leave it and come here as quickly as possible. There is no place in the world where a man meets so rich a reward for conduct and industry.

In 1773 he married Elizabeth Hayes Ellison. That same year, representatives from the thirteen American colonies set up the Continental

Congress in order to work towards setting up an American republic, and Dunlap played an important role in the American Revolution.

John Dunlap was so supportive of the colonies' rights that he co-founded and subsequently became an officer in the First Troop of Philadelphia City Cavalry, and saw action with George Washington as his bodyguard at the Battles of Trenton and Princeton. He continued in the cavalry after the war, rising to the rank of major in command during the 'Whiskey Rebellion'.

It was factors such as these that contributed to the revolutionary leaders approaching Dunlap to print the Declaration of Independence and the Articles of Confederation. On 2 July 1776, the Second Continental Congress voted to declare independence, and on 4 July, they agreed to the final wording of the American Declaration of Independence.

That evening John Hancock requested Dunlap print broadside copies of the agreed-upon declaration that was signed by him as President and Charles Thomson as Secretary. It is thought that Dunlap printed as many as 200 broadsides that were distributed to the members of Congress; these have since become known as the 'Dunlap Broadsides', which were the first published versions of the Declaration.

In 1777 he took over the printing of the Journals of the Continental Congress from Robert Aitken, but lost the contract only two years later after printing in his newspaper a letter from Thomas Paine that leaked news of the secret French aid to the Americans.

This episode may have influenced Dunlap's decision to temporarily withdraw from public life. He was wealthy enough to do so. By combining public pursuits with his printing business, Dunlap was able to establish a substantial fortune. An astute businessman and speculator, Dunlap's major financial success came from land acquisition in Kentucky and Virginia. During the American Revolution, he bought property confiscated from Loyalists who refused to take Pennsylvania's new loyalty oath.

DID YOU KNOW?

Today there are only about twenty-five of the Dunlap broadsides that are known to exist – dispersed among American and British institutions and private owners. A Dunlap broadside – unsigned, as it is known, sold for $8.14 million, the highest price ever achieved to date for an object sold at an Internet auction. This copy was discovered in 1989 by a man browsing in a flea market who purchased a painting for $4 because he was interested in the frame. Concealed in the backing of the frame was an original Dunlap broadside.

By 1795, when he was 48 years of age, Dunlap was able to retire permanently from business with a sizable estate. He died of 'apoplexy' in Philadelphia on 29 November 1812 and was buried with full military honours at Christ Church, Philadelphia.

GENERAL JAMES SHIELDS: THE ALTMORE MAN WHO CHALLENGED ABRAHAM LINCOLN

Did you know that a Tyrone man once challenged the famous Abraham Lincoln to a duel? The person in question was General James Shields, an American politician and United States Army officer who was born in Altmore, a small hamlet located between Dungannon and Carrickmore.

Shields was born in Altmore on 12 December 1810 and came from a wealthy family who owned the Altmore Loan Fund Building. He was well educated and became fluent in four languages – and after enjoying several adventures as a sailor, the teenager decided to stay in America.

Shields eventually settled in Kaskaskia, Randolph County, Illinois where he studied and later practised law. The young emigrant Shields took part in the Black Hawk War in the early 1830s, and in 1836 was elected to the State legislature. He served as a member of the State House of Representatives, then as a State Supreme Court justice and later in 1839 as the State Auditor.

It was during this period that Shields nearly fought a duel with Abraham Lincoln on 22 September 1842. Lincoln had published an inflammatory letter in a Springfield, Illinois newspaper, the *Sagamon Journal* that poked fun at Shields. Lincoln was a Whig and Shields was a Democrat and the two had often clashed rhetorically in the past.

Taking offence at the article, Shields demanded 'satisfaction' and the incident escalated to the two parties meeting at Sunflower Island, near Alton, Illinois to participate in a duel. Just prior to engaging in combat, accomplices of the two men intervened and were able to convince Lincoln and Shields to cease hostilities, on the grounds that Lincoln had not written the letters.

> **DID YOU KNOW?**
>
> James Shields (as a Democrat) is the only person in United States history ever to serve as a Senator for three different states: Senator from Illinois 1849 to 1855, from Minnesota from 11 May 1858 to 3 March 1859, and from Missouri from 27 January 1879 to 3 March 1879.

Instead of changing the course of history, the two eventually became good friends. Shields later became one of Abraham Lincoln's civil war generals in the 1860s, and famously inflicted a tactical defeat of the Confederate General, Thomas 'Stonewall' Jackson during the Battle of Kernstown, Virginia in 1862.

Shields had also served as a brigadier general during the Mexican War. He led a brigade of volunteer troops during the drive from Veracruz to Mexico City. Shot through the lung, at Cerro Gordo in April 1847, he was breveted to major general for his conduct in that battle, Shields' distinguished political and military career was impressive and, but for the fact that he was born in Ireland, he might well have been the Democratic candidate for the United States Presidency during the mid-nineteenth century.

James Shields died in Ottumwa, Iowa on 1 June 1879 after having served only three months as a Senator for Missouri. He is buried in St Mary's Cemetery, Carrollton, Missouri. A statue of this celebrated man was the second to be erected in Washington's Hall of Fame – the first being to none other than George Washington, the first United States President.

SOME OTHER NOTABLE TYRONE PEOPLE

Sir Guy Carleton: born in Strabane, emigrated to Canada and rose to the rank of Governor. He successfully challenged an invasion of Canada by the American colonies in 1776.

John Foster McCreight: the first premier of British Columbia, a western province of Canada, was born in Caledon in 1827. With his distinguished legal background, he also became a justice of the Supreme Court of British Columbia.

Cecil Frances Alexander: hymn writer and poet, born in Dublin in 1818, she lived in both Castlederg and Strabane at various times during her life. Some of her hymns, such as the renowned 'All Things Bright and Beautiful', 'There is a Green Hill Far Away' and the Christmas carol

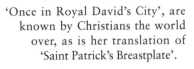

'Once in Royal David's City', are known by Christians the world over, as is her translation of 'Saint Patrick's Breastplate'.

James Dilworth: was born in Donaghmore, but left Ireland as a young man and eventually settled in New Zealand in 1841. He later established the Dilworth Trust, a large charity which assists families with their education costs.

Joseph McGarrity: was born in Carrickmore but emigrated to the United States in 1892 at the age of 18 and settled in Philadelphia. From 1893 until his death he was a leading member of Clan na Gael – an Irish Republican organisation in the United States during the late nineteenth and twentieth centuries. He also was a successful businessman; he founded the *Irish Press* newspaper that supported the War of Independence in Ireland.

7

TYRONE'S SPORTING
SUCCESS STORIES

This chapter takes a look at some of the players, managers, teams and facilities involved in a range of sports played in Tyrone – and indeed there are many outstanding Tyrone sporting success stories. This includes individuals such as Dennis Taylor and Darren Clarke who have won international sporting events, while teams such as Dungannon Rugby and the Tyrone Gaelic footballers have won All-Ireland titles.

In terms of team sports, the most popular countywide team sports in County Tyrone include Gaelic football, soccer and rugby, while basketball, hockey and cricket are popular in various parts of the county.

GAELIC GAMES IN COUNTY TYRONE

Gaelic games covers a number of sports, and perhaps the most popular sport in County Tyrone is Gaelic football. There are forty-eight football clubs of varying sizes throughout the county with the Tyrone county teams enjoying a high profile thanks to their continuing success, the sport continues to appeal to thousands of players and spectators each year.

Whilst the Gaelic Athletic Association was founded in Thurles, County Tipperary in 1884, it wasn't until twenty years later – in January 1904 – that Tyrone were properly organised with a county board administrative structure. Its chairman was Michael O'Nolan from Strabane – the father of Tyrone's most famous writers, Brian O'Nolan (see Chapter 8). That same month, the first Tyrone team competed in the Ulster Senior Football Championship, but were defeated by Armagh.

The early decades of the Association in Tyrone were relatively quiet, with better organisation in the east of the county, and only eight championships were completed until 1920. While Gaelic football was (and has since been) the predominant Gaelic game in Tyrone, there is plenty of evidence to suggest that hurling thrived in certain areas, especially in Strabane – where a team (*Lámh Dhearg* – or 'Red Hands') from the town represented Tyrone in an Ulster Senior Hurling Championship game as early as 1903.

Arguably the first great breakthrough in Tyrone came with the winning of the first All-Ireland title in Gaelic football, at minor level in 1947; the title was defended successfully the following year. Some of these players graduated to play their part in the first ever Ulster Senior Championship-winning team of 1956, when the mighty Cavan were defeated.

This historic breakthrough led to a real belief that Tyrone could compete with the very best teams in Ireland, and while Tyrone continued to win Ulster titles, the ultimate success – the All-Ireland Senior Football title (or Sam Maguire Cup as it is better known) – continued to elude Tyrone teams including narrow defeats in the 1986 and 1995 finals.

That all changed on 28 September 2003: a hugely significant date in the history of Tyrone GAA, as the county's senior football team won the All-Ireland senior football title for the first time. Managed by Mickey Harte and captained by Peter Canavan – both from the Errigal Ciaran club – Tyrone defeated Ulster neighbours Armagh in the final by 0–12 to 0–9 at Croke Park, Dublin. This was the first final that involved teams from the same province following the introduction of the 'qualifier' system two years previous, where teams defeated in an earlier round had another chance of progression.

The Tyrone team that played in that historic final was: John Devine (Errigal Ciaran), Ciaran Gourley (Rock), Cormac McAnallen (Eglish), Ryan McMenamin (Dromore), Conor Gormley (Carrickmore), Gavin Devlin (Ardboe), Philip Jordan (Moy), Kevin Hughes (Killeeshil), Sean Cavanagh (Moy), Brian Dooher (Clann na nGael), Brian McGuigan (Ardboe), Gerard Cavlan (Dungannon), Enda McGinley (Errigal Ciaran), Peter Canavan (Errigal Ciaran), Owen Mulligan (Cookstown).

Subs used in the All-Ireland Final: Stephen O'Neill (Clann na nGael) for Brian McGuigan, Brian McGuigan for Peter Canavan, Colin Holmes (Armagh Harps) for Ciaran Gourley, Peter Canavan for Gerard Cavlan, Chris Lawn (Moortown) for Conor Gormley.

Other panellists: Pascal McConnell (Newtownstewart), Dermot Carlin (Killyclogher), Mark Harte (Errigal Ciaran), Paul Horisk (Errigal Ciaran), Peter Loughran (Errigal Ciaran), Seamus Mulgrew (Donaghmore), Declan McCrossan (Owen Roe O'Neill's Leckpatrick), Michael McGee (Loughmacrory), Cormac McGinley (Errigal Ciaran), Frank McGuigan (Ardboe), Brian Robinson (Donaghmore), Michael Coleman (Ardboe), Ryan Mellon (Moy).

A decade later, there was another landmark event to symbolise the progress made by the GAA in the county. The magnificent new Garvaghey complex located between Ballygawley and Omagh was officially opened after years of intense planning and building.

The £7 million complex incorporates a 43-acre site that includes five grass pitches, a full-sized 3G surface, a multi-purpose training area, an auditorium, fully equipped gyms and meeting rooms. It is an excellent investment for future generations of Tyrone 'Gaels'.

A Tyrone Gaelic Football Legend: Frank McGuigan

Frank McGuigan is widely regarded as one of the most naturally gifted footballers to ever play the game of Gaelic Football, he captained Tyrone to a Senior Ulster Championship title in 1973 when he was aged 19. It was his outstanding performance in the 1984 Ulster Final against Armagh at Clones when he scored 11 points from play that remains one of the great feats of the sport. Five off the right foot, five off the left, and one fisted over the bar ensured legendary status for the Ardboe O'Donovan Rossa clubman.

Since that inaugural success in 2003, Tyrone have won the All-Ireland title on two further occasions – in 2005 and 2008; with Kerry defeated on both occasions in the final by Mickey Harte's team. Tyrone is now recognised as one of the top teams in Gaelic football, with the hope of more success in the years ahead.

Club Structure

The club structure in Tyrone Gaelic football reflects the parochial strength of the county. There are three divisions in Tyrone club football – Senior, Intermediate and Junior – incorporating almost fifty clubs; it is extremely competitive.

The O'Neill Cup for the Tyrone Senior Football Championship is the pinnacle for club teams, with the final taking place each autumn – usually at Healy Park in Omagh. There is real pride in an area and a parish when a club team wins, and the celebrations can last for months!

The club structure also serves the other Gaelic sports well, with hurling clubs competing for the Benburb Cup, while camogie and ladies' football continues to grow on an upward curve thanks to the success of club and county teams in the past decade.

SOME SELECTED GAELIC GAMES MILESTONES IN COUNTY TYRONE:

1929: The first recorded penalty kick in Gaelic football (thanks to recently discovered footage) is by Malachy Mallon from Eglish, playing for Tyrone against Antrim at O'Neill Park Dungannon.

1963: Jack Martin from Omagh is the first referee from Tyrone to officiate at an All-Ireland Football Final – the minor final between Kerry and Westmeath. He also refereed the Under-21 Finals in 1965 and 1966.

1972: Paddy Devlin from Omagh referees the All-Ireland Senior Football Final replay between Offaly and Kerry; he also referees the 1974 Senior final between Dublin and Galway.

1980: Kevin McCabe from Clonoe becomes the first 'All-Star' winner for the county; the Tyrone camogie team wins an Ulster Junior Championship for the first time.

1986: The first person to score a goal for Tyrone in the All-Ireland Senior Football Final is Paudge Quinn from Ballygawley against Kerry in 1986.

1992: Carrickmore Ladies win the inaugural Ulster Club Football Championship.

1993: Errigal Ciaran becomes first Tyrone winners of the Ulster Senior Football Club Championship.

1997: St Patrick's Academy Dungannon becomes the first team from Tyrone to win the All-Ireland Colleges' Hogan Cup.

1995: Tyrone hurlers win their first ever Ulster Junior Championship title.

2007: Greencastle St Patrick's becomes the first Tyrone side to win an All-Ireland club title at Croke Park, defeating Duagh of Kerry in the junior final.

2004: The Cormac McAnallen Cup for International Rules Football is named in honour of the late Eglish and Tyrone footballer who also represented Ulster and Ireland with great distinction.

2014: The Tyrone senior hurling team wins the Nicky Rackard Cup for the first time, defeating Dublin side Fingal at Croke Park Stadium.

A Tyrone Gaelic Football Legend: Peter Canavan

For a lengthy period in the 1990s and early 2000s, Peter Canavan was acclaimed by many GAA supporters as being the most complete footballer in Ireland; his recognised skills and excellent technique made him one of the finest players of the modern era.

Canavan was fast-tracked to play senior inter-county level football after arriving in a blaze of glory from the lower age ranks, where he won two consecutive All-Ireland Under-21 medals in the early 1990s. A winning run with Tyrone at senior level in 1995 culminated in an Ulster title and a narrow All-Ireland Final defeat to Dublin, 1–10 to 0–12.

Peter scored 11 of those points for Tyrone, and went on to receive recognition for his efforts in the 1995 season by winning the Footballer of the Year award. (He also won a total of six All-Star Awards during his distinguished playing career.)

The following year was another successful one for Tyrone, claiming another provincial title. Unfortunately in the All-Ireland Semi-Final defeat against Meath, Canavan sustained a leg injury that would affect his playing career.

Barren years followed for Tyrone until 2001, although Canavan continued to inspire other teams that he represented such as his club and province to further honours. A batch of talented young players had arrived on the scene by this stage and together with Canavan and more experienced players, Tyrone enjoyed All-Ireland successes in 2003 and 2005 – with Canavan the team captain for that historic breakthrough.

Peter Canavan had a huge influence in these finals; contributing five points against Armagh in the earlier final after a clever use of his abilities by manager Mickey Harte, and scoring an important goal against Kerry just before half-time, setting Tyrone on their way to victory in the 2005 final. Peter Canavan announced his retirement from the inter-county game shortly after that final, but he remains involved within the GAA both in a coaching capacity and as a media pundit.

RUGBY IN COUNTY TYRONE

Rugby is another popular sport in Tyrone, and the county has supplied many players to the Ulster and Ireland teams over the decades. This included Omagh-born Thomas Thornhill who made four appearances for Ireland, his first coming in 1892.

Thomas had the honour of becoming the president of the Irish Rugby Football Union (IRFU) in 1901 – he wasn't the first Tyrone person to hold that honour. In fact, James Hamilton, the Duke of Abercorn, based at Baronscourt near Newtownstewart, was the first ever IRFU President, holding the position between the years 1874–76.

Dungannon was the sixth rugby club formed in Ireland (in 1873) and was a founder member of the IRFU. It was also one of the first towns in Ireland to form a rugby club, possibly due to the growing influence of the Royal School's rugby team in the town.

The Royal School won the prestigious Ulster Schools Cup in 1907, defeating Belfast Inst. in the final. The 'Royal' have reached the final on four other occasions, with the most recent being in 1975. Another Tyrone school, Omagh Academy, reached the final in 1985.

George McAllen

This Royal School Dungannon pupil was picked to play for Ireland at fullback aged just 17 in 1896 – the first schoolboy ever to be honoured for the Irish Rugby team. He played against Scotland in that landmark game, and retained his place in the team for the next outing against Wales – but after that never played again for his country.

All-Ireland Success

Following his retirement from the playing side of the game, Dungannon legend Willie Anderson was appointed head coach of Dungannon Rugby Club in 1995 and his objective was to win the newly-formed All-Ireland League. Anderson recruited some of the best players throughout the province and beyond, with Irish internationals Justin Fitzpatrick, David Humphreys and Jonathan Bell all joining the Dungannon project.

The powerful combination resulted in the Stevenson Park side becoming the first team from Ulster to win the All-Ireland league title in May 2001, after a final victory against Munster side Cork Constitution by 46 points to 12 at Lansdowne Road.

The Dungannon team was: Bryn Cunningham, Jan Cunningham, Ryan Constable, Jonathan Bell, Tyrone Howe, David Humphreys, Stephen Bell, Justin Fitzpatrick, Nigel Brady, Gary Leslie, Paddy Johns, Aidan Kearney, Alastair Boyd, Tony McWhirter and Andrew Hughes.

As a result of winning the All-Ireland League, Dungannon has now won every major domestic competition in Ulster and Ireland: The All-Ireland League Division One (2001) and Division Two (1992), the All-Ireland Floodlit Cup, The Stevenson Shield (Ulster Senior League), The Ulster Senior Cup, The Ulster Towns Cup, The Ulster Junior Cup and The Forster Cup.

The town of Dungannon also has strong connections to New Zealand rugby. Uchter Knox, the Earl of Ranfurly (who was the Governor-General of New Zealand from 1897 to 1904 and previous to that was the president of Dungannon Rugby Club) presented the Ranfurly Shield to the New Zealand Rugby Football Union in 1901, and it remains a prestigious trophy in New Zealand's domestic Rugby Union competition.

Dungannon Rugby Club's ground, Stevenson Park, was purchased in 1969, and just prior to the famous All-Ireland League win in 2001, the first phase of a redevelopment of its facilities was completed. The venue is named after Robert Stevenson, a member of the family who owned the Moygashel Linen Mills and also an Irish rugby international who won fifteen caps between 1887 and 1893. He also played for Royal School Dungannon and later became president of the Irish Rugby Union, following in the footsteps of Thomas Thornhill.

Other Tyrone teams such as Clogher Valley, Omagh and Strabane compete in the Ulster regional leagues. Clogher Valley and Omagh have both enjoyed great success in the Ulster Towns Cup in recent decades, with Omagh winning the title in 2002, while Clogher Valley have won titles in 2007, plus two-in-a-row in 2011–12.

A Tyrone Rugby Legend: Willie Anderson

Sixmilecross-born Willie Anderson enjoyed a distinguished rugby playing career, making twenty-seven appearances in the lock position for Ireland between 1984 and 1990. He was also a key member of the successful Ulster Rugby team that dominated the Irish inter-provincial series during the 1980s and represented the British and Irish Lions. Anderson captained Ireland during the inaugural Rugby World Cup in 1987.

In November 1989, the conquering New Zealand All Blacks visited Dublin for an international test match. Despite their fearsome reputation, the world champions didn't scare Willie as captain of the Irish team – and during the New Zealander's traditional pre-match haka routine, Willie cajoled his team mates into standing firm against the men in black and confronting the haka. The Ireland team linked arms and stood toe-to-toe with their opponents – receiving much publicity for doing so!

Despite Ireland losing the game by 23 points to 6 after a gutsy display, they gained respect for their unorthodox approach to playing the All Blacks. The Irish coach that day in 1989 was another Tyrone man, Jimmy Davidson from Donaghmore, who was also supportive of the idea. And while some media commentators criticised the perceived disrespect towards the visitors (who had never been challenged performing the haka), others marvelled in a unique approach to playing the best side in the world.

SOCCER IN COUNTY TYRONE

It's often been difficult for soccer to compete with the other popular team sports in Tyrone; however, at one point during the 1990s, the county could boast two senior football teams, with Dungannon Swifts and Omagh Town based in the Irish League Premier Division.

Dungannon Swifts

Dugannon Swifts were founded in 1949, and the club managed a notable feat when they entered and won the Mid-Ulster Shield on their first attempt. After twenty years in the Mid-Ulster League, in the early 1970s the Swifts were promoted to the Irish League 'B' Division.

The year 1975 saw Stangmore Park become the official home of the football club when they bought the land in the Stangmore area of the town. In the 1980–81 season, Dungannon had one of their most successful years ever and were crowned runners up in the old 'B' Division Championship.

One of their greatest achievements came during the 1987–88 season as they showed their skills in the Mid-Ulster Senior Cup by defeating Irish League high-flyers Glenavon 2–1 to bring the trophy to Stangmore Park.

In 1997, Dungannon Swifts were elected to the Irish League First Division for the first time – and they have consolidated their status as Tyrone's premier club side in recent years with a number of eyecatching results. In May 2007 the team reached the final of the Irish Cup for the first time ever, but were denied the silverware by Linfield who won 3–2 on penalties following a 2–2 draw after extra time at Windsor Park in Belfast.

Based at the St Julian's Road ground, Omagh Town were elected to the Irish League in time for the 1990–91 season, and enjoyed five seasons before a relegation to the First Division. The 'Town' enjoyed success in 1999–2000, winning the First Division trophy and had the privilege of playing English Premiership sides Liverpool, Manchester United and Arsenal to raise money for the victims of the Omagh Bombing.

As Omagh Town are no longer in competitive football, Dungannon Swifts are now the only Tyrone representatives in the Irish League Premier League. However, Castlederg-based Dergview are in the second tier of the Northern Ireland Football League – known as Championship One – while Coagh United are in the third tier – Championship Two.

Soccer has a thriving grassroots league structure across Northern Ireland, and local leagues such as the Fermanagh and Western League include Tyrone teams Drumquin United and Strabane Athletic.

The county has produced some excellent players, such as Aaron Hughes and Niall McGinn, in recent years to the professional leagues in England and Scotland, and who have also represented Northern

Ireland. Gerry Armstrong, arguably Tyrone's most famous soccer export, was the scorer of the most famous goal by a Northern Ireland player – against hosts Spain in the 1982 World Cup. He was born in Fintona and played at club level for Tottenham Hotspur in England and Real Mallorca in Spain.

Tyrone at the Milk Cup

Teams from County Tyrone have successfully competed in the Milk Cup international youth tournament based in Counties Antrim and Derry for the past three decades – with a number of impressive results along the way.

The county is represented at Junior (Under 14) and Premier (Under 16) levels each year. In 2005, Tyrone famously beat the Paraguay national team 1–0. This is just one of many impressive results gained by a Tyrone team over the years, and in 2013 the Tyrone Premier team reached the final – only to be defeated by Manchester United.

A Tyrone Soccer Legend: Aaron Hughes

Once a Milk Cup competitor, Cookstown native Aaron Hughes, joined Newcastle United as a 15-year-old, and made his first team debut in November 1997 as a substitute for the English Premiership side in a Champions League game against Barcelona in the Nou Camp stadium!

Completely unfazed about this remarkable progress, Aaron made his international debut at the age of 18 in a 1–0 defeat of Slovakia in March 1998. He had established himself as a regular for the St James Park side by season 2000–01, becoming an assured presence in the right-back position. Aaron made over 200 appearances for Newcastle United before transferring to Aston Villa.

In the latter part of his career he moved again to London side Fulham – helping the Craven Cottage side reach the Europa Cup Final in 2010. Aaron became captain of the Northern Ireland team in April 2002 – and played a key role in the superb victories at Windsor Park over England and Spain in 2005 and 2006 respectively.

Internationals

A selection of Tyrone players to have represented Northern Ireland at soccer:

Gerry Armstrong (Fintona)
Aaron Hughes (Cookstown)
Allan Hunter (Sion Mills)
Victor Hunter (Sion Mills)
Niall McGinn (Donaghmore)
Pat Sharkey (Omagh)
Ivan Sproule (Castlederg)

SOME OTHER TEAM SPORTS

Basketball

There has been a strong tradition of basketball in Dungannon since the 1950s, and the current club, Tyrone Towers, is the largest basketball club in Ireland outside of Belfast and Dublin. They currently field eight teams, ranging from primary school age to senior ladies and mens.

Cricket

Cricket has traditionally been a popular sport in the north-west Tyrone area. The Sion Mills club was formed back as 1864, and was the venue of Ireland's most impressive cricketing moments when, in July 1969, Ireland beat a touring West Indian team including Clive Lloyd, who was soon after to become a highly successful West Indies captain. Ireland bowled the 'Windies' out for 25 in the first innings, before scoring 125 for 8 declared.

Ossie Colhoun

Ossie Colhun from Sion Mills was a member of the Ireland team that defeated the West Indies in 1969. He made eighty-seven appearances as a wicketkeeper for the Ireland team between 1959 and 1978. In one international match he had 7 dismissals (all catches) while his overall total of dismissals for Ireland was 186, which included 42 stumpings.

Hockey

Cookstown Hockey Club is the flagbearer for Tyrone in the Ulster and Ireland leagues though there are teams in the other three main towns – Dungannon, Omagh and Strabane.

Formed in 1951, Cookstown has both male and female teams and among the many great players who have represented the club is Martin Sloan. He played for Ireland 149 times and was captain in more than 100 games, while his fellow clubman Andy Barbour won eighty-four caps and scored 12 goals for Ireland. The Cookstown club has won the Irish Senior Cup on two occasions (1986–87 and 2010–11) and the Ulster Senior League on five occasions.

INDIVIDUAL SPORTS

Snooker, darts, golf and bowls are popular individual sports in Tyrone. There have been some incredible accomplishments by Tyrone people participating in these sports.

DENNIS TAYLOR

This native of Coalisland emigrated to Blackburn, England in the 1960s and developed his promising snooker career that had shown so much potential in Gervin's snooker club, turning professional in 1971. This potential was finally realised in 1985 when he became the World Snooker Champion, defeating the reigning champion Steve Davis in an epic final watched by more than 18 million people on television.

This final set many records and has been regarded by many as the greatest game of snooker ever seen. At fourteen hours and fifty minutes long it broke the record for the longest thirty-five-frame snooker match. Reigning champion Davis had led by 8 frames to 0 at one stage, and even when he gained a 17–15 lead, Taylor won the following 2 frames to level the contest with just one frame to play.

In a dramatic finale, Davis led 57–44 but – having missed a series of chances and Taylor capitalising on this – the stage was set for a 'black ball fight'. Davis over-cut the black and left Taylor with the opportunity to pocket the final ball and claim snooker's ultimate prize, and 'cue' wild celebrations in Tyrone. He remains the only Tyrone person to have achieved such a feat.

Taylor remained in the Top 16 World Rankings for over twenty years and also won the Irish Snooker Championship six times (1980–82) and (1985–87), the 1984 Rothmans Grand Prix and the 1987 Benson and Hedges Masters. Alongside Alex Higgins and Eugene Hughes, Taylor played a pivotal role in Ireland's three Snooker World Cup wins (1985–87). He retired from playing professionally in 2000 and currently works as a television commentator on the game.

DARREN CLARKE

The Dungannon man is one of the world's best-known golfers. During a highly successful career he has been a magnificent role model for County Tyrone on golf's world stage. Clarke developed his early skills on the fairways and greens of Dungannon Golf Club.

He turned professional in 1990, and his big breakthrough came ten years later when he won the Matchplay Championship – which netted him the $1 million first prize.

Three weeks after the death of his wife Heather in August 2006, Clarke was chosen as one of the 'wild cards' for the Ryder Cup at K Club in County Kildare. He produced one of his most memorable performances, earning 3 points for his European team which was instrumental in the final success.

In 2010 he beat a world-class field in the JP McManus Invitational Pro-Am at Adare Manor in Ireland, where he had a one shot victory over Luke Donald. Clarke finished 30th in the European Tour Race to Dubai, assuring his place in the field for the 2011 Open Championship at Royal St Georges.

It was then that he enjoyed his finest hour, as he claimed a major championship in July 2011. Clarke won the 140th Open Championship at Royal St George's in Kent by three shots from American golfers Phil Mickelson and Dustin Johnson, rounding off an amazing three days of golf to secure the coveted first 'major' title. At the age of 42, Clarke was the oldest Open Champion since Roberto de Vicenzo in 1967.

DID YOU KNOW?

Darren Clarke was a member of five consecutive European Ryder Cup teams between 1997 and 2006 – winning on four occasions and was also appointed as a non-playing vice-captain in 2010.

COOKSTOWN 100

Organised by the Cookstown and District Motorcycle Club, the main route of the popular 'Cookstown 100' motorbike race is situated in the Orritor area outside the town, and is held annually each April.

It's an incredibly fast track as most of the road races are, with several jumps along the way and a couple of sharp 90-degree corners, including Mackney Corner and McAdoo Bends. It's a race with a lot of history behind it; the first race was in 1922.

The winners from County Tyrone in recent decades include Phelim Owens from Dungannon, while Ryan Farquhar, also from Dungannon, had the distinction of winning five races at the Cookstown 100 in one day. During a record-breaking season in 2009 season, Farquhar surpassed Joey Dunlap's total of 118 Irish National Road Race wins.

His trademark bright orange and black colours and number 77 became his trademark – and he retired from road racing in September 2012 following the tragic death of his uncle and mentor, Trevor Ferguson, during the Manx Grand Prix.

HANDBALL

Part of the Gaelic games family, handball is a competitive game in which either hand or fist may be used to serve and return the ball off a wall.

Handball is immensely popular in rural areas of Mid-Tyrone, and the Carrickmore and Loughmacrory areas are among those that have produced a number of outstanding exponents of the sport. The year 2012 was particularly successful for the game in Tyrone, as four All-Ireland titles were won by Tyrone players in the Juvenile grade – a new record for the county.

BOXING

Boxing is a popular sport and boxing clubs prominent around the county include Clonoe and Kildress. Tyrone has produced two Olympians:

In Rome 1960, Danny O'Brien from Omagh beat Esteban Aguilera of Cuba in the first series but then lost to Silver Medallist Sandro Lopopolo of Italy in the second series.

Twenty-four years later, Tommy Corr from Clonoe represented Ireland at the 1984 Olympics in Los Angeles. He won his first bout against Arigoma Mayero from Zimbabwe but lost the second to Nigerian Jeremiah Okurodudu.

8

CREATIVE TYRONE

Creative Tyrone people have enhanced the life and soul of the county with their excellent contributions; their work has been read widely, listened to, and appreciated in places near and far. The chapter also looks at the current centres within the county that showcase art, literature, music and other forms of culture.

LITERATURE: THE WRITERS

There have been a number of writers of plays, poetry and novels that have been recognised for their work not just locally within Tyrone, but throughout the world. Often inspired by the beautiful landscapes of their native county, recurring themes for some of these writers include emigration – as in the case of John Montague's poetry – and the question of tradition and modernity – often featured in Brian Friel's plays.

William Carleton

According to his autobiography, William Carleton was born in a peasant cottage in the townland of Prillisk in the Clogher Valley on 4 March 1794. Carleton's family were bilingual; his father was an accomplished storyteller of old Irish tales and historical anecdotes, and his mother knew traditional Irish songs. William's early education entailed attending a succession of hedge schools, but his family were evicted in 1813 and William joined a secret society known as the 'Ribbon Men' for a short time.

He had been originally interested in becoming a priest, but a pilgrimage to Lough Derg convinced him that he wasn't cut out for clerical life. He instead became a wandering tutor and focused on recording and writing the experiences of the Irish rural people and their customs – most famously published in one volume in *Traits and Stories of the Irish Peasantry* (1830) (see Chapter 4). Some of his stories were even based on his own life experiences. Most importantly, this work was valuable as it provided an insight into Irish country life in pre-famine times.

He spent the latter part of his life in Dublin, and under the influence of Revd Caesar Otway joined the Church of Ireland for a time. He wrote a powerful tale of the Irish Great Famine in 1847 – *The Black Prophet* – and was working on his autobiography at the time of his death in January 1869.

Visitors to the Clogher area can now view Carleton's Cottage – the novelist's childhood home. There is a popular annual literary festival held in August in the Clogher Valley that celebrates the work of Carleton and explores themes such as migration and literary links between Ireland and Scotland.

William Collins

Born in Strabane in 1840, William Collins emigrated to Canada at the age of 15, where, after some years as a labourer, he developed an interest in poetry and literature. He enlisted in the Federal Army and fought in both the American Civil War and in the Fenian raid of Canada.

On his return to Cleveland, Ohio, Collins wrote many articles and poems for the press, achieving widespread acclaim in the process. He coined the phrase 'Among the Bushes', and in 1874 he went to New York where he worked on the editorial staff of the *Irish World* and eventually went on to hold an executive post on the *New York Tablet*.

Polly Devlin

Hailing from Ardboe, Devlin is a member of a creative family, as her brother Barry is a member of *The Horslips* Celtic rock band, while her sister Marie Heaney (a teacher and writer) is the widow of Nobel Laureate Seamus Heaney.

Devlin was Features Editor of *Vogue* Magazine in London, New York and Paris during the 1960s – interviewing personalities such as John Lennon and Andy Warhol. In 1983, she wrote *The Far Side of the Lough*, a widely acclaimed collection of fictional stories based on her own childhood on the shores of Lough Neagh. She also wrote *All of us There*, a book that explores the relationships between her family, and the landscape around them.

Brian Friel

Brian Friel was born in 1929 in Killyclogher; his father was a schoolmaster from Derry and his mother a postmistress from Glenties, County Donegal. Friel's maternal grandparents were Irish speakers from Donegal who would prove influential in his work. His early education at St Columb's College, Derry proceeded to St Patrick's College, Maynooth, where he studied for a career in the priesthood.

Friel would eventually decide to follow his father into teaching and taught mathematics to primary and secondary school pupils during the 1950s. His first major success stage success, *Philadelphia, Here I Come*, was the undisputed hit of the Dublin Theatre Festival in 1964.

Many of his later plays, including *Dancing at Lughnasa*, were set in Ballybeg, a rural settlement in remote Donegal. Other well-known plays by Friel include *Volunteers* (1975), *Living Quarters* (1977), *Translations* (1980) and *Dancing at Lughnasa* (1990).

In 1980, Friel co-founded the Field Day Theatre Company with actor Stephen Rea. They staged *Translations* as their first production in Derry's Guildhall. This celebrated play was concerned with the mapping of Ireland by the Ordnance Survey in the 1830s – which became a key theme in the debate on traditional and modern values in Ireland.

In 1983 Friel was awarded an Honorary Doctorate of Literature by the National University of Ireland. He was appointed to the Seanad Éireann in 1987 and served until 1989. That year, BBC Radio launched a 'Brian Friel Season', a six-part series devoted to his work, and he was the first living playwright to receive such an honour.

The Brian Friel Theatre and the Brian Friel Centre for Theatre research was opened by Brian Friel in 2009 at Queen's University Belfast. The Brian Friel Centre aims to produce world-class research as well as offering students a vibrant environment in which to study.

Benedict Kiely

Benedict Kiely was born near Dromore on 15 August 1919; his family moved to neighbouring Omagh when he was only a year old, and this is where he spent his formative years. His father was a Boer War veteran, who later worked as a survey measurer for the Ordnance Survey. Benedict was educated at Mount St Columba's by the Christian Brothers. In the spring of 1937, he left Omagh and began a new life in County Laois, where he decided he would train as a Jesuit priest. It was after a lengthy recuperation from a spinal ailment that he decided he wasn't suited towards a religious vocation.

He enrolled for an arts degree at University College Dublin (UCD), where he was involved in the production of a poetry broadsheet and was a member of the literature society. By the time his first novel, *Land*

Without Stars, was published in 1946, Kiely was writing for the *Irish Independent*. During this time he also completed a study of the works of William Carleton. In 1950 he resigned, as the banning of his novel *In a Harbour Green* (1949) had not endeared him to the management.

Following this, a positive review he wrote of George Farquhar's *The Recruiting Officer* prompted complaints from readers and Kiely was no longer asked to review plays. The banning of two further books, *Honey Seems Bitter* and *There Was An Ancient House*, led Kiely in later years when asked about censorship to reply, 'If you weren't banned, it meant you were no bloody good.'

He then worked for *The Irish Press*, where he spent almost fifteen years as literary editor. He retired from full-time journalism in the mid-1960s, became a visiting professor of creative writing at several American universities, and later lectured at UCD.

Kiely was awarded honorary doctorates by the National University of Ireland and the Queen's University, Belfast. In 1996 he received the highest honour of Aosdána, the Irish artists' body, when he was elected a Saoi in recognition of his contribution to literature.

On 9 February 2007, Benedict Kiely died in Dublin after a short illness at the age of 87. The inception of the Benedict Kiely Literary Weekend earlier that decade has continued annually every September and is currently held in Omagh's Strule Arts Centre.

W.F. Marshall: The 'Bard of Tyrone'

Reverend William Forbes Marshall was a Presbyterian minister renowned for his contribution to poetry during the first half of the twentieth century. Born on 8 May 1888 in Drumragh, a few miles outside Omagh, he was the second of Mary and Charles Marshall's three sons.

Marshall first attended Sixmilecross National School, of which his father was the principal. He was further educated at Royal School Dungannon, for which his poem, 'R.S.D.' has been adopted as the school song and is sung on speech day and other special occasions.

Blue plaque at
Sixmilecross Presbyterian Manse

Marshall graduated in the arts from Queen's College Galway (an associate college of the Royal University of Ireland) in 1908. During his time in the west of Ireland, he displayed the first signs of his prowess as a poet, with 'D'Arcy's Point' and 'Alma Mater' believed to be written during his time in Galway.

Following his initial degree of success, he began a theological course along with his elder brother at the Presbyterian College in Botanic Avenue, Belfast. Marshall was ordained and installed in Aughnacloy, County Tyrone on 26 June 1913, but less than three years later a call to his home congregation, Sixmilecross, was accepted and he was installed there on the 20 April 1916.

Later that year he married Susan McKee of Belfast. The family remained in Sixmilecross until May 1928, when Marshall was installed in Castlerock Presbyterian Church in County Derry. Serving as a minister at Castlerock for over thirty years, his publications became more prolific during his time spent there. Marshall composed poems such as 'Hi Uncle Sam', 'Me An' Me Da', 'Sarah Ann' and 'Our Son'.

W.F. Marshall's poems were collated and published in the form of four books: *Verses from Tyrone, Ballads and Verses from Tyrone, Ballads from Tyrone* and *Tyrone Ballads*. Noticeably these four books of poems all contain the name of his native county in the title; and not surprisingly he was dubbed the 'Bard of Tyrone' as a result of this. Many of these poems are written in a Tyrone dialect, including 'Me An' Me Da' which includes the lines of the first stanza:

I'm livin' in Drumlister,
An' I'm getting very oul'
I have to wear an Indian bag
To save me from the coul'.
The deil a man in this townlan'
Wos claner raired nor me,
But I'm livin' in Drumlister
In clabber to the knee.

Reverend Marshall's published work is not confined to poetry. A series of talks entitled *Ulster Speaks* was broadcast and later published by the BBC. Indeed over several decades the BBC broadcast a series of talks on dialect by him.

A prolific writer and poet, Marshall's other publications include a novel, *Planted by a River*, and *Ulster Sails West* (a history of eighteenth-century Ulster emigration to the United States that appeared just as American GIs were landing in Ulster during the war).

Appointed Lecturer in Education at Magee University College in Derry City in 1932, Marshall was well equipped to fill this post because of his command of expressive language. Before one *Ulster Speaks* series, broadcast in 1935, he said, 'Dialect is the museum in which students of English can check and trace the progress of English.'

Through his work, Marshall became a leading authority on Mid-Ulster English (the predominant dialect of Ulster). His distinct interest in the Ulster dialect led him to produce a dialect version of Shakespeare's *A Midsummer Night's Dream* which was broadcast by the BBC.

W.F. Marshall died on 27 January 1959, leaving behind a valuable and extensive written legacy. Twenty-four years later, in 1983, *Livin' in Drumlister: The Collected Ballads and Verses of WF Marshall* was published and within three years the book had sold 11,000 copies.

John Montague

This Irish-American poet was born in Brooklyn, New York in 1929, but was sent at the age of 4 to live with his aunts in Garvaghey, a townland located between Ballygawley and Omagh. He went on to become a lecturer in universities such as Berkeley in California and University College Cork. His epic work *The Rough Field* brought him to the attention of many. It showed the significance of Garvaghey in his life, and portrayed it as a microcosm of the Northern Irish 'Troubles'.

Windharp
(for Patrick Collins)
The sounds of Ireland,
That restless whispering
You never get away
From, seeping out of
Low bushes and grass,
Heatherbells and fern,
Wrinkling bog pools,
Scraping tree branches,
Light hunting cloud,
Sound hounding sight,
A hand ceaselessly
Combing and stroking
The landscape, till
The valley gleams
Like the pile upon
A mountain pony's coat.

> (John Montague, 'Windharp', *New Collected Poems* (2012), by
> kind permission of the author and The Gallery Press

Paul Muldoon

The poet and academic Paul Muldoon was born in 1951, and grew up near Moy on the Tyrone/Armagh border. He studied English at Queen's University, Belfast – where he was taught by Seamus Heaney. After graduation, Muldoon worked as a radio producer for the BBC in Belfast, before moving to the United States in 1987. He now lives in New Jersey where he is a Professor in the Humanities at Princeton University.

He has produced more than thirty collections of poetry, including: *New Weather*, *Mules*, and *The Annals of Chile*. In 1993, he won the Pulitzer Prize for Poetry for *Moy Sand and Gravel*. Paul Muldoon has won many other prestigious awards including the T.S. Eliot Prize.

Brian O'Nolan

An iconic master of satire, Brian O'Nolan was born in Strabane in 1911 and became known as one of the most important Postmodernist writers in twentieth-century Ireland. However, it has only been in recent years that his works have been appreciated by a wider audience.

He worked under a number of pseudonyms, most famously Flann O'Brien (his English novels) or Myles na gCopaleen (in Irish); and was renowned for his expertise in both languages. Among his most successful works include: *At Swim-Two-Birds*, *The Third Policeman* and *The Poor Mouth*.

O'Nolan was born into an Irish-speaking family, and spoke only Irish until he was 6 years old. O'Nolan's childhood has been described as happy, though somewhat insular, as the language spoken at home was not that spoken by their neighbours.

The O'Nolan family endured something of a nomadic existence during the first few decades of the century; originally from Strabane, moving to Glasgow, then to Tullamore in County Offaly, before finally settling in Dublin in 1925. It was there that O'Nolan took up study in UCD. During his college days he discovered a gift for debate and a great talent for writing. One of his group of friends in UCD was the Dungannon poet Charlie Donnelly who died in Jarama in 1937 during the Spanish Civil War.

The two Tyrone men were prominent contributors to the student publication *Comhthrom Féinne* (Fair Play), O'Nolan writing under the pseudonym Brother Barnabas. In 1934 this prodigious group of writers began to publish a short-lived magazine called *Blather*.

Despite all the distractions, O'Nolan graduated from UCD with a Master of Arts degree; the completed thesis being on the subject of 'Nature in Irish Poetry'. O'Nolan decided to follow in his father's footsteps by becoming a civil servant. Almost simultaneously with his entry into the Civil Service came the beginning of *At Swim-Two-Birds*. Published in 1939, it sold just 244 copies before the London warehouse in which it was stored was destroyed in the Blitz.

Another novel that gained much notoriety was *The Third Policeman*. It was again characterised by its bizarre humour. Its mixture of styles, a hallmark of the book, produces some fine comic moments, as when a verse in the style of ancient Irish mythology is added:

When money's tight and is hard to get
And your horse has also ran,
When all you have is a heap of debt –
A PINT OF PLAIN IS YOUR ONLY MAN.

As Myles na gCopaleen, O'Nolan published a regular column entitled *'Cruiskeen Lawn'* (Irish for 'the little full jug') in *The Irish Times*, usually in English, but sometimes in Irish, sometimes in Latin and sometimes in a strange English-Irish hybrid of his own invention. The columns introduce a regular set of characters, such as the *'PLAIN PEOPLE OF IRELAND'*.

O'Nolan originally got the chance to write the column by starting a series of literary arguments with himself in the letters page of *The Irish Times*, and fighting them out from behind a wall of pseudonyms. The editor, after indulging this for some time, tracked him down and offered him a job.

Having satirised a government minister in the column, O'Nolan was forcibly retired from the Civil Service in 1953. He continued to write a number of newspaper articles using different names than before and by the early 1960s wrote his final two novels: *The Hard Life* (1961) and *The Dalkey Archive* (1964). Neither of these are as well regarded as his earlier works, however. Brian O'Nolan died on 1 April 1966.

CULTURAL CENTRES

In the past few decades, a number of new arts facilities have opened up throughout Tyrone. Here is a brief look at some of the arts, heritage and performance venues throughout the county:

Dún Uladh Cultural Heritage Centre, Killyclogher

'The Fort of Ulster' is the provincial headquarters of Comhaltas Ceoltóirí Éireann, for the Meitheal Regional Centre which incorporates Counties Antrim, Derry, Donegal, Down and Tyrone. It serves as a centre for those who wish to develop a deeper awareness of Ireland's ancient cultural heritage. From early in the year the centre plays host to Irish dance, music, song and drama.

Craic Theatre, Coalisland

This unique venue is built on the site of an old weaving factory and supported by a mixture of local volunteers and sponsors. It is a dedicated community arts facility that promotes music, dance, drama and crafts.

Bardic Theatre, Donaghmore

Situated in the village of Donaghmore, the Bardic Theatre Group has entertained thousands of people in the Mid-Ulster area and beyond over the past three decades. Its award-winning productions have included *High School Musical*, *Blood Brothers* and *The Diary of Anne Frank*.

Strule Arts Centre, Omagh

This purpose-built arts facility is located in the town centre, on the site of the former Town Hall and is continuing the tradition of arts and culture in Omagh. The Strule Arts Centre forms part of a wider regeneration project for the High Street/George Street/Riverside area of Omagh Town Centre, and first opened its doors to the public in June 2007 for an inaugural performance.

Burnavon Arts and Cultural Centre, Cookstown

Seating up to 350 people, the Burnavon's main auditorium is a popular venue for concerts and performances, and offers a wide range of arts and entertainment. The Cookstown Tourist Office is also based in the Burnavon Centre.

Alley Arts and Conference Centre, Strabane

The Alley is an impressive theatre complex, art gallery and conference centre based in Strabane. It is now recognised as one of the leading arts and conference venues within the north-west of Ireland. It is a fully equipped auditorium with seating for up to 270 people.

Ranfurly House Arts and Visitor Centre, Dungannon

This venue has had a long and interesting history – originally opened as a bank building in the nineteenth century, it also was formerly the headquarters of 'Irish World' Heritage Centre which specialised in genealogical research.

It now houses a visitor information service, an arts centre and a permanent multi-media interpretative exhibition area which narrates the story of the Flight of The Earls and Plantation of Ulster. A performance area known as 'The Square Box' is located on the upper ground floor and can seat up to ninety-eight people theatre style.

An Creagán Visitor Centre

Music and storytelling has been a part of life in the area surrounding An Creagán for centuries, as neighbours visited each other to céilí for entertainment. This cultural centre, situated just off the main road between Cookstown and Omagh, does its part to keep these traditions alive by providing regular cultural events such as storytelling nights and poetry exhibitions. It also houses an interpretative exhibition and offers cultural guided tours of the surrounding area.

Kinturk Cultural Centre, Moortown

The history of the Lough Neagh fishing and eel industry is featured in this centre based in Moortown in East Tyrone. There are also displays of old traditional boats and equipment.

MODERN PUBLIC ART SCULPTURES

Strabane has become a key centre for public art in County Tyrone, much of it in the past decade thanks to the inspiration of the Millennium Sculpture in the town.

The Millennium Sculpture: Let the Dance Begin

Comprised of five semi-abstract figures each 18ft in height, this sculpture created by Maurice Harron represents two traditions and cultures merging.

Installed to mark the millennium, tourists still flock annually to get their picture taken with Ireland's tallest musicians – affectionately known as 'The Tinnies' – at 18ft in height. Music and dance are represented by two dancers, a musician on the Lifford side holding a fiddle and another musician on the Strabane side with a fife.

Ambrose the Pig

Standing outside the Alley Arts and Conference Centre is an 8ft tall bronze pig named Ambrose. Among the influences for his design are beliefs held in Celtic times that pigs represented fertility and prosperity, and were accordingly held in great reverence. Sculpted by Martin Heron, Ambrose is named after a character which features in the works of Brian O'Nolan/Flann O'Brien.

The popularity of these led to a host of others, including a sculpture of the writer Brian O'Nolan outside Strabane Library. The *HEART* sculpture trail in the North West includes *The Flax Spinner* in Sion Mills, and a *Sport Sculpture* in Donemana. These provide an important insight into the rich heritage and culture of the area.

This recent interest in public art work is certainly not confined to North Tyrone, with the Dungannon and Cookstown areas also proudly displaying some degree of public art work. The approach roundabout to Cookstown has a sculpture which takes its inspiration from the Sperrin Mountains and the Beaghmore Stone Circles.

Its near neighbour, Dungannon town centre has a new public art scheme beside the 'Hill of the O'Neills' called 'Timeline' which celebrates the historical and modern significance of Dungannon by taking the viewer on a visual journey from the earliest settlement up to the present day and beyond.

CREATIVE MUSICAL PERFORMERS

Country music is particularly popular in Tyrone, and it can boast an internationally famous musician:

Philomena Begley

Known as the 'queen' of Irish country music, Philomena's career has now spanned more than five decades. Born and raised in Pomeroy, her first venture as a singer was with the popular Old Cross Céilí Band, after a friend had dared her to get up and sing!

This proved to be both a brave and wise decision and Begley was asked to officially join the band. Their first 'gig' was in Ardboe on 11 May 1962.

The group soon became known as the Old Cross Bandshow and released three records in Ireland during 1968 and 1969. In September 1970, the band changed its name to The Country Flavour. Begley's first record hit following this became her first chart hit when 'Here Today, Gone Tomorrow' reached number 7 in the Irish Chart.

Philomena and her husband Tom Quinn formed The Ramblin' Men in 1974 and regularly toured with Ray Lynam, and they recorded many duets together. Probably their most popular was 'My Elusive Dreams', which is mentioned in The Pogues' 'A Pair of Brown Eyes'. During that year, Begley had a hit with her version of Billie Jo Spears' hit song 'Blanket on the Ground' which took her to number 5 in the Irish Charts; this fared better in Ireland than Spears' version in the charts!

By 1977 she had began to make an impact in the American market and commenced a major tour of the United States. The following year Begley was invited to sing at the 'Grand Ole Opry' with Porter Wagoner. She has appeared with the likes of Don Williams and George Jones at this venue.

Her career has gone from strength to strength and a compilation of her music, *The Philomena Begley Collection*, has now sold more than 100,000 copies worldwide. This achievement was fittingly marked with a presentation of a gold disc during a special concert in Ardboe in May 2012 – fifty years after her debut with the Old Cross Céilí Band.

Paul Brady

This singer songwriter is one of Ireland's most popular musicians. Born and raised in Strabane, he was receptive to a wide variety of music from an early age. Influenced by the music of the 1950s and '60s era, he learned to play the piano, and by the age of 11 he had begun to play guitar.

It was from the mid-1960s, as a student in UCD, that he began to develop as a singer and performer joining a succession of RnB acts; fronting his own band Rockhouse, covering the songs of Ray Charles and James Brown – and blues legends like Chuck Berry.

The renewal of interest in Irish traditional music gave birth to the first wave of Irish ballad groups like The Clancy Brothers, The Dubliners, and The Johnstons, Brady joined the latter band with whom he recorded seven albums.

Moving with The Johnstons in January 1969 to live in London and later in 1972 to New York City, he returned to Dublin a few years later to join Planxty, a popular Irish folk band of the early '70s. This band helped to launch the solo careers of artists such as Andy Irvine and Christy Moore.

During the mid-1970s Paul Brady played as a duo with Irvine, a relationship which produced *Andy Irvine and Paul Brady*, a popular album. In 1978, Brady released a solo record, *Welcome Here Kind Stranger*. This helped him establish his popularity and reputation as one of Ireland's best interpreters of traditional songs.

Surprising most observers at the time, Brady departed from the Irish folk music genre and released *Hard Station* in 1981. While the record

---

DID YOU KNOW?

1992 Eurovision Song Contest Winner Linda Martin (with the song 'Why Me') started off her musical career when she joined the band Chips in Omagh in 1969. They quickly became one of the top bands in Ireland on the live circuit and released hit singles 'Love Matters', 'Twice a Week' and 'Goodbye Goodbye' during the mid to late 1970s.

wasn't a 'commercial success' it did help to bring his music to an international audience.

The albums which followed, such as *True For You* (1983), *Primitive Dance* (1987), and *Spirits Colliding* (1995) collectively established Brady as the pre-eminent Irish singer-songwriter of his generation. Gradually other artists worldwide began to record his songs, such as Cher and Tina Turner.

Throughout his career Paul Brady has worked and collaborated with other artists, and in 2000, *Oh What a World* was a successful partnership with Carol King and Ronan Keating – hailed as one of his best ever records.

A decade later, Paul released his 14th solo album, *Hooba Dooba*, to widespread acclaim. This came just a year after his recognition by the University of Ulster of his services to traditional Irish music and songwriting by the awarding of the honorary degree of Doctor of Letters.

Jimmy Kennedy

The popular song-lyricist Jimmy Kennedy was born in Omagh in 1902, but his family moved to Coagh in the east of the county a few years later as his father (a member of the Royal Irish Constabulary) was posted there. He attended Cookstown Academy and was later educated at Trinity College, Dublin.

He became an officer in the Colonial Service, but feeling unfulfilled by this career, began writing songs as a sideline. Thanks to this decision, he enjoyed astonishing success with 'The Teddy Bear's Picnic' which sold 4 million records. He also devised the novelty dance 'The Hokey-Cokey' which was popular during victory celebrations in the aftermath of the Second World War.

TRADITIONAL MUSIC AND SONG

This is another popular form of music in Tyrone, and among the most celebrated musicians of the form was Geordie Hanna (1925–1987) from Derrytresk, near Coalisland. His songs were from the 'loughshore tradition' such as 'Old Ardboe' and 'The Fisher's Cot'.

A well-known traditional music group also from the east of the county were 'Four Men and a Dog', founded by the skilled Tyrone fiddle and banjo player Cathal Hayden. Their first CD release was 'Barking Mad'; the influential Omagh-born guitar player and producer Artie McGlynn was also important to their success, establishing a reputation as one of the world's best interpreters of traditional Irish music on guitar.

9

TYRONE TRIVIA AND AN ABC OF TYRONE

Tyrone is sometimes referred to as being 'Among the Bushes' – a phrase created by William Collins; but it is also known as the 'Red Hand County'. This is especially the case among Gaelic games followers – the term is proudly displayed on the Tyrone GAA jersey.

Sometimes known as 'The Red Hand of Ulster', the symbol is rooted in Irish Gaelic culture. Its origins are said to be attributed to the mythical Irish figure Labraid Lámh Dhearg (Labraid of the Red Hand) from the Uí Neill clan.

A number of common myths are associated with the origin of the significance of the Red Hand. According to one myth, Hugh O'Neill was inspired to adopt the symbol after seeing a hand on the Monasterboice high cross and being told that it represented the hand of God supporting the Christian Church.

Perhaps the better-known story is when a member of the O'Neill clan – thought to be Labraid – was racing a rival across a stretch of water to claim a piece of land. In a desperate bid to be first he cut off his hand and threw it on to the shore – enabling the O'Neill to claim the land.

Another variation of this story concludes that it was none other than Niall of the Nine Hostages who severed his own hand in order to win his crown from his brother.

The Red Hand symbol remains popular in County Tyrone; it is featured on the O'Neill family coat of arms – and is also present on other Ulster counties such as Antrim, Cavan and Monaghan.

The Red Hand is one of the few cross-community symbols to be used and adopted in Ulster, with many sporting clubs and organisations (including Ulster GAA, rugby and hockey) all adopting it.

Historically, it was used by Unionists in the 'Ulster Solemn League and Covenant' in September 1912, while, due to its perceived roots as a Gaelic and Irish symbol, Nationalist groups such as the Ancient Order of Hibernians and the Irish Citizen Army also adopted it in the early twentieth century.

TYRONE TRIVIA

The tallest structure in Ireland is the mast of the Strabane Transmitting Station, which provides UHF Television and Digital (DAB) Radio services to the Strabane area. Transmission mast stands at a height of 333 yards.

The geographical centre of Ulster lies between the villages of Pomeroy and Carrickmore.

The village of Moy was designed by Lord Charlemont after Bosco Marengo in Piedmont, Italy. When he returned from his Grand Tour in the 1760s he was so impressed by the Italian town that he decided to build an Irish replica. A Twinning Partnership between the two areas was formally agreed on 27 August 1997.

The 53rd Ulster Fleadh (traditional music festival) was held in Dromore during July 2013.

The *Tyrone Constitution* newspaper was established in 1844, making it the oldest newspaper in the county, and one of the longest-running in the whole of Ireland.

A new flood wall in Strabane was built by a Belgium firm in 1989 at a cost of £7 million.

A well-known Tyrone proverb to consider: a Tyrone woman will never buy a rabbit without a head for fear it's a cat!

The Church of the Good Shepherd in Sion Mills is based on the design of a church at Pistoia, near Florence in Italy.

Emigrants from the Ardboe area often took with them a small chip of stone from Ardboe Cross to remind them of home.

Songwriter Jimmy Kennedy attended Cookstown Academy at the same time as the Nobel Prizewinner for Physics in 1951, Ernest Walton. Remarkably a school photograph was taken where the two are seated together.

CASTLEDERG AND THE WEATHER

Castlederg has been prominent in recent years for being a point of reference for the weather in north-west Tyrone. During the harsh winter of 2010, a new record regional minimum temperature of -18.7C was set at Castlederg, on the morning of 23 December (the record had fallen twice in four days).

FIVE RECOMMENDED TYRONE-RELATED WEBSITES

Tyrone Tribulations www.tyronetribulations.com
This tongue-in-cheek website lampoons people and places in Tyrone, and has proven quite popular in its appeal to online users who can follow the progress of people and events on a daily basis. Among the most creative and eye-catching headlines are:

Poetry in critical state in Tyrone
Valentine competition 'cat'
Mixed reaction in Tyrone to Eurovision disaster
Greencastle, Kildress, Gortin and Donemana call for relocation of Sperrins

Teamtalkmag www.teamtalkmag.com
An impressive website that comprehensively covers the Gaelic games scene in Tyrone.

Flavour of Tyrone www.flavouroftyrone.com
This food tourism website has many recommendations for locals and visitors to the county.

Roots Chat www.rootschat.com
RootsChat is a community of people who help each other with their family history. It has many millions of postings and hundreds of

thousands of members worldwide. Tyrone has its own forum for added convenience.

The Tyrone Association in Dublin www.tad.ie

Since its foundation in 1956, *Muintir Thír Eoghain* (The Tyrone Association Dublin) has promoted fellowship between Tyrone people of all walks of life resident in and around Dublin city. It is now a much more social and cultural organisation, which organises events to raise money for charities based in Tyrone.

TYRONE'S RECORDED POPULATION SINCE 1600: SELECTED YEARS

Year	Population
1600	20,000
1666	37,000
1712	70,277
1744	77,493
1749	63,666
1753	89,382
1791	180,385
1821	261,865
1831	304,468
1841	312,956
1851	255,819
1861	238,500
1871	215,766
1881	197,719
1891	171,401
1901	150,567
1911	142,665
1926	132,792
1937	127,586
1951	132,082
1961	133,919
1971	139,073
1981	143,884
1991	157,570
2011	177,986

It is interesting to note that in 1841, when Tyrone's recorded population peaked at 312,956 – this was more than double the population of the first recorded census of the twentieth century, in 1901 when 150,567 people lived in Tyrone. This sharp decline continued due to factors such as emigration but the pattern changed significantly in the post-Second World War era – and the population of the county has been climbing steadily ever since.

MOST POPULAR BABY BOYS' NAMES BY LOCAL GOVERNMENT AREA IN TYRONE, 2013

Area	Name
Cookstown	Charlie/James
Dungannon	James
Omagh	James
Strabane	James

MOST POPULAR BABY GIRLS' NAMES BY LOCAL GOVERNMENT AREA IN TYRONE, 2013

Area	Name
Cookstown	Aoife
Dungannon	Aoife
Omagh	Anna/Sophie
Strabane	Emily

SAINTS ASSOCIATED WITH TYRONE

St Patrick

St Patrick, whose feastday is celebrated on 17 March, is a particularly popular name associated with schools, churches and sporting teams throughout the whole of Ireland, and this applies especially to County Tyrone, where it is believed his influence was considerable.

It is claimed that he founded a number of monasteries and churches in the county; in the case of Dungannon, the reverence held for St Patrick's life and work is clearly apparent – as there are three schools and one church named after the patron saint in the town:

St Patrick's College (Dungannon)
St Patrick's Academy (Dungannon)
St Patrick's Primary School (Dungannon)

St Patrick's Breastplate
Christ be with me, Christ be before me
Christ be behind me, Christ be within me
Christ be beneath me, Christ be above me
Christ be at my right, Christ be at my left
Christ be in the fort, Christ be in the chariot
Christ be in the ship
Christ be in the heart of everyone
Who thinks of me
Christ be in the mouth of everyone
Who speaks to me
Christ be in every eye that sees me
Christ be in every ear that hears me.

St Macartan

St Macartan's feastday is exactly a week after that of St Patrick, on 24 March, and this is appropriate given he was the companion and bodyguard for Patrick on his missions into pagan territory.

He was consecrated bishop by Patrick and assigned to the druidic stronghold of Clogher. After founding the church at Clogher, Patrick preached for three days and three nights at a nearby place called Lemain – and Brigid (Macartan's niece) fell asleep during his preaching!

The Church of Ireland Cathedral in Clogher is named after St Macartan – the present building was erected on the site in 1744.

TWIN TOWNS

Some of the main towns in County Tyrone are twinned with other towns in Europe and North America:

Cookstown: Plérin-sur-mer (France)
Omagh: L'Haÿ-les-Roses (France)
Strabane: Zeulenroda-Triebes in the state of Thuringia (Germany) and Sioux Falls, South Dakota (USA)

SOME TYRONE POLITICAL 'FIRSTS'

Bernadette Devlin

Bernadette Devlin became the youngest women ever elected to Westminster; she was also the first female Member of Parliament to represent a Tyrone-related constituency in Westminster.

In April 1969, Devlin was elected to Westminster as the 'Unity' candidate for Mid-Ulster, defeating the Unionist candidate by 4,211 votes in a poll of 92 per cent. She was initially involved in the civil rights campaign as a member of the People's Democracy movement.

She took her seat in parliament on her twenty-second birthday, and increased her majority to nearly 6,000 in the general election of June 1970, before losing her seat to Unionist candidate John Dunlop in the February 1974 general election.

Austin Currie

Austin Currie was at the time the youngest ever Member of Parliament returned to Stormont when he was elected as a Nationalist in a 1964 by-election in East Tyrone. As an SDLP representative, he served as a government minister in the power-sharing executive at Stormont (1974) as Head of the Department of Housing, Planning and Local Government.

He later served in Dáil Éireann (from 1994–1997) where he became Minister of State at the Departments of Education, Justice and Health. In so doing, he became the only former member of Dáil Éireann to have served in the Northern Ireland Parliament at Stormont.

Thomas James Clarke

Clarke was born on the Isle of Wight to Irish parents on 11 March 1857. His father, James Clarke from County Leitrim, was a sergeant in the British Army. The family moved to Dungannon when Thomas Clarke was 7 years old. Clarke was the first signatory of the 1916 Proclamation of the Irish Republic and one of the leaders during the 1916 Easter Rising in Dublin, and was executed for his role in it.

MEMBERS OF THE FIRST NORTHERN IRELAND ASSEMBLY (1998) IN COUNTY TYRONE-BASED CONSTITUENCIES

Fermanagh South Tyrone:
Tommy Gallagher (SDLP)
Sam Foster (UUP)
Gerry McHugh (SF)
Michelle Gildernew (SF)
Joan Carson (UUP)
Maurice Morrow (DUP)

Mid-Ulster:
William McCrea (DUP)
Martin McGuinness (SF)
Denis Haughey (SDLP)
Francie Molloy (SF)
John Kelly (SF)
Billy Armstrong (UUP)

West Tyrone:
Oliver Gibson (DUP)
Pat Doherty (SF)
Joe Byrne (SDLP)
Barry McElduff (SF)
Derek Hussey (UUP)
Eugene McMenamin (SDLP)

FAMOUS PEOPLE WITH TYRONE AS A CHRISTIAN NAME

Tyrone Power
An Irish American film and theatrical actor. Born in Cincinatti, Ohio in 1914, Tyrone Power served in the Marine Corps during the Second World War. He returned to act in a series of Hollywood movies, including his starring roles in *The Razor's Edge* (1946) and *Witness for the Prosecution* (1957).

Tyrone Guthrie
An English theatrical director. The Tyrone Guthrie Centre is now based at his family ancestral home at Annaghmakerrig near Newbliss in County Monaghan.

Tyrone Davis

An American soul singer born in Greenville, Mississippi. He enjoyed a successful career and had three number 1 hit songs including 'Turning Point' in 1975.

INFAMOUS TYRONE PEOPLE

William Burke

William Burke was born in Clady, close to the Donegal border. In 1818, he moved to Scotland to work on a canal, and by 1827 he was living in a lodging house in Edinburgh kept by William Hare, originally from Derry.

Burke and Hare sold for dissection the body of an elderly person who had died in the house. They received £10 from Dr Robert Knox of Edinburgh University, and in the next few years they disposed of at least fifteen people by intoxicating and then suffocating them and selling them to Dr Knox.

In 1828, neighbours became suspicious when Marjorie Campbell disappeared and her corpse turned up in Dr Knox's house. On 28 January 1829, on the evidence of Hare, Burke was found guilty of murder and hanged in Edinburgh.

William Greer

During the 50th anniversary of the John F. Kennedy assassination, the story of this Stewartstown native came to prominence thanks to the local media. William 'Bill' Greer emigrated to North America in 1929 and later became an agent of the United States Secret Service. He is best known for having driven President John F. Kennedy's automobile in the motorcade through Dealey Plaza in Dallas on the fateful day of 22 November 1963.

'Typhoid' Mary Mallon

Mary Mallon was born in 1869 in Cookstown and emigrated to New York City at the age of 14. Working as a cook, her misfortune began in August 1906 when typhoid fever broke out at a summer home in Oyster Bay, New York.

The house's owner hired a sanitary engineer named George Soper to investigate how the fever started. It transpired that Mallon had been hired just a week before the outbreak of typhoid fever but had subsequently disappeared from the home. Soper eventually tracked Mallon down in March 1907 at a Park Avenue home – and where a case of Typhoid had been reported. She was arrested despite her pleas of ignorance, and tests proved she was a carrier of the typhoid bacterium, though she herself was immune to it.

The press soon labelled her 'Typhoid Mary' and she was quarantined in an isolated hospital for three years. One of the conditions of her release was that she would abstain from cooking. But Mallon couldn't resist and under the alias of Mary Brown she gained employment in another New York hospital – and typhoid fever broke out again. She was sent back to the isolated hospital where she lived out the rest of her life. It is thought that Mallon may have infected as many as 1,400 people, and gained notoriety for the wrong reasons in New York.

SOME TYRONE-BORN SCREEN ACTORS PAST AND PRESENT:

Gerard McSorley (Omagh): Acted in *Braveheart* and *Angela's Ashes*.
Sam Neill (Omagh): Acted in *The Hunt for Red October* and *Jurassic Park*.
Birdie Sweeney (Dungannon): Acted in *The Snapper* and *Ballykissangel*.

TEN COMMON SURNAMES IN TYRONE AND THEIR ORIGIN

Quinn

Quinn is the single most popular name in Tyrone. The O'Quinns were an important sept of the *Cenél nEógain*. They were part of the Clann Feargusa, descendants of Fergus, son of Eoghan, son of the fifth-century Niall of the Nine Hostages, founder of the Uí Neill dynasty. Their name is derived from Coinne, a grandson of Fergus. The septs of Clan Fergus acquired extensive lands to the south of the Sperrin Mountains, around Tullaghoge.

O'Neill

A well-documented family name in Tyrone, the O'Neill clan claims descent from both Conn of the Hundred Battles and Niall of the Nine Hostages – the fifth-century High King of Ireland. Eoghan, son of Niall, gave his name to the *Cenél nEógain*, of whom the O'Neills were the chief sept.

The first to take O'Neill as their surname was Domhnall, who took the name of his grandfather Niall killed in a battle with the Vikings. O'Neill thus translates as 'grandson of Niall'.

Some O'Neills from Tyrone you may have heard of:

Owen O'Neill (Cookstown): writer, actor.
Stephen O'Neill: Gaelic football star.

The blind harper Arthur O'Neill (1737–1816) coined the saying: 'Wherever an O'Neill sits is always the head of the table.'

Arthur was born in the townland of Drumnastrade near Dungannon. When 2 years of age he accidentally suffered an injury to his right eye while, he said, 'diverting myself with a penknife.'

Kelly

This is the second most popular surname in the whole of Ireland (after Murphy) and derives from 'descendant of Ceallach'. There are at least seven distinct septs of O'Kelly in Ireland. One particular sept claims descent from the fourth-century Colla-da-Críoch, King of Ulster.

Donnelly

The O'Donnellys were a *Cenél nEógain* sept, the name is derived from '*Donn*' meaning 'brown-haired' and '*gal*' meaning warrior. Whilst the Donnelly clan trace their lineage to Eogan, son of Niall of the Nine Hostages, the O'Donnelly sept originated in Donegal, they moved to Tyrone and settled in Baile Uí Dhonnghaile (Donnelly's Town) – now known as Castlecaulfield.

Some Donnellys from Tyrone you may have heard of:

Daniel O'Donnelly (Strabane): a member of the Patriot Parliament in 1689
Patrick Modardha O'Donnelly: during the Irish Rebellion of 1641, Patrick captured the castle of Ballydonnelly from Lord Caulfield – and when the castle was retaken Ballydonnelly was renamed Castle Caulfield.

Devlin

Known in Irish as the ÓDoibhilin clan, their native territory was 'Muintir Dhoiblin' (now Muintirevlin in the Parish of Ardboe). The Devlins traced their descent from Muireadach Mac Earca, son of Muireadach, son of Eogan who ruled that territory on the west shore of Lough Neagh.

A Devlin from Tyrone you may have heard of:

Joe Devlin: although born in Belfast, it is thought he had family connections with the East Tyrone area. Whilst he was an MP at Stormont, he also represented counties Fermanagh and Tyrone at Westminster.

Wilson

Wilson is among the thirty most common names in Ireland, and as an English name is one of the derivatives of William, and means 'son of Will'. It is estimated that as many as four-fifths of Wilsons living in the historic province of Ulster are of Scottish ancestry. Many Scottish families entered Ireland through the port of Derry during the seventeenth and eighteenth centuries and settled in the Foyle Valley which includes areas of County Tyrone.

Murphy

Murphy is indeed the most numerous name in Ireland; and Irish people in the Irish diaspora have often been labelled the surname as a generic term of affection or sometimes derision.

The majority of Tyrone Murphys were originally a *Cenél nEógain* sept '*MacMurchada*' – meaning 'descendant of Murchadh' a personal name meaning 'sea warrior'. This clan controlled the rich lands of Muintir Birn in South Tyrone and their territory was bounded by the barony of Truagh in County Monaghan; however, they were driven out of the region by the O'Neills and many settled in the south of Armagh under O'Neill of the Fews.

A Murphy from Tyrone you may have heard of:

John Murphy (1812–80): from Omagh, founded the theological publishing house of Murphy and company in Baltimore.

Stewart

This is one of the most common non-Irish names in Tyrone, and is derived from the old English *stigweard*, a 'keeper of the house' and an honourable position. Many people with the surname migrated to Tyrone and other Ulster counties during the Plantation. Andrew Stewart, Lord Ochiltree of Ayrshire, was one of the nine Scottish chief undertakers of the Plantation; his grandson William was created Lord Mountjoy in 1682.

A Stewart from Tyrone you may have heard of:

Joe Stewart: Member of Parliament for Fermanagh and Tyrone, elected in 1934.

MacCullagh

This surname is also spelled McCulloch or McCullough (although more often in other Ulster counties such as Antrim and Down), and many of this Tyrone clan originate from Scotland. It has been suggested that the MacCullagh name is derived from the Scots Gaelic *Mac Cullaich* meaning 'son of the boar' but it could also originate from the Ulster Gaelic *Mac Con Uladh* which means 'Son of the Hound of Ulster'.

A MacCullagh from Tyrone you may have heard of:

James MacCullagh: mathematician.

Campbell

The name is derived from the Scots Gaelic *Caimbeul*, meaning 'wry mouth' and it is thought that the Campbells in the county could be descended from a branch of the Scottish clan, the Galloway MacCampbells.

However, many of the Tyrone Campbells were members of the Tyrone sept Mac Cathmhaoil, derived from '*cathmhao*l' meaning 'battle chief', tracing their lineage to Eogan, son of Niall of the Nine Hostages. At the height of their power in the twelfth century from their base at Clogher, they controlled a large portion of Tyrone.

Some Campbells from Tyrone you may have heard of:

Robert Campbell: from the townland of Aughalane near Plumbridge, he emigrated to America in 1822 and became a bank president in St Louis, Missouri. His childhood home has been recreated in the Ulster American Folk Park.

10 POPULAR VISITOR ATTRACTIONS IN COUNTY TYRONE

Blessingbourne Carriage and Costume Museum, Fivemiletown
Grant Ancestral Homestead, near Ballygawley
An Creagán, Omagh
Ambrose the Pig, Strabane
Ranfurly House Arts & Visitor Centre, Dungannon
Dungannon Park
William Carleton's Cottage, Clogher
Lissan House, Cookstown
Ulster American Folk Park, Omagh
Knockmany Passage Tomb Heritage Site, Augher

FAMOUS CLERGYMEN ASSOCIATED WITH TYRONE

Doctor Patrick O'Donnelly: The Legend of the Bard of Armagh
While the nature of this book is concerned with people, places and events relating to Tyrone, the anomaly that was the 'Bard of Armagh' needs some explanation.

Patrick O'Donnelly was born in the parish of Desertcreat, near Cookstown in 1649. He became known as the Bard of Armagh; an outlawed priest during penal times.

Several members of the O'Donnelly clan came to Desertcreat in 1610 due to the confiscation of their lands (due to the Plantation of Ulster) which were located in the nearby parish of Donaghmore. Patrick O'Donnelly decided to join the Catholic priesthood; it is believed that he spent the three years before his ordination in the Drogheda school, founded in 1670 by Archbishop Oliver Plunkett.

O'Donnelly first curacy was in Armagh, where he remained until he went to study in Paris, earning a doctorate in law around 1679. On his return, the archbishop appointed him Bishop of Dromore, County Down before moving to parishes in County Armagh.

Working in the disguise of a wandering minstrel, he assumed the guise of Phelim Brady, the Bard of Armagh, as he had took refuge in the area of Slieve Gullion in South Armagh, overlooking Newry. As to the origin of the assumed name, it is believed that in the village of Stradone in Laragh Parish, County Cavan lived a schoolmaster called Fiachra Mac Brady. It is likely that this much-travelled teacher met O'Donnelly travelling in disguise through the country, and that the bishop assumed the surname Brady to avoid detection by the authorities.

Often the bishop offered Mass in secret; in mountain passes, on the Mass Rock, or at his favourite spot, the 'lone bush' near his 'Doctor's Quarters'. As a result of the penal laws, priests and bishops had to travel incognito and because of their lack of numbers had to cover a very wide area. He travelled on foot in Counties Tyrone, Derry, Louth, Armagh and Down, guiding and advising the priests and people whom he met. For a time in the early part of the eighteenth century, O'Donnelly was the only remaining Catholic bishop in Ireland. He remained in the Doctor's Quarters until his death in 1716 at the age of 66.

He was laid to rest in his native parish and family grave at the site of what is now Desertcreat Parish Church, near Cookstown. This graveyard holds the remains of many Penal Day priests and O'Donnelly's reputed burial place is locally known as the 'Bard's Grave'.

Cardinal Joseph MacRory
Born near Ballygawley in 1861, he was one of ten children of Francis and Rose MacRory. He attended school at Glencull and then went on to study at Armagh and Maynooth. He was ordained a priest in 1885 and became the first president of St Patrick's Academy Dungannon. Appointed Bishop of Down and Connor in 1915, he signed a declaration against conscription (mandatory service in the military) due to the First World War. It was also during his time based in Belfast that he presented a trophy for the annual Gaelic football competition between schools – which still thrives: The MacRory Cup. He was elevated to Archishop of Armagh and Primate of All-Ireland in 1928 before being created Cardinal by Pope Pius XI the following year.

Father Patrick O'Loughran
Born in the parish of Donaghmore during the sixteenth century, O'Loughran became a priest and later a chaplain to the Earl of Tyrone Hugh O'Neill and his household. After the Flight of the Earls in 1607,

O'Loughran was arrested and charged with helping O'Neill make his escape and of giving sacraments to the exiled noblemen. In his trial he denied all charges of treason and argued that he was being persecuted for his faith. He was found guilty and sentenced to death in 1612. On 27 September 1992, Patrick O'Loughran, along with sixteen other people from different parts of Ireland, was beatified by Pope John Paul II.

Bishop William Alexander

The Church of Ireland Bishop of Derry and Raphoe and his wife, the author of hymns Cecil Frances Alexander, lived at Milltown House, Strabane. He was the author of numerous theological works, while his collected poems were published in 1887 under the title of *St Augustine's Holiday and Other Poems*. William Alexander was the last Irish bishop to sit in the Westminster House of Lords before the disestablishment of the Church of Ireland in 1871.

Reverend George Walker

The Church of Ireland rector was known as the 'Defender of Londonderry' for his role as joint governor during the Siege of Derry in 1689, and had helped form a regiment of troops under Lord Charlemont. However, previous to this he succeeded his father (Revd George Walker senior) as rector of the parish of Donaghmore. The east window of St Michael's Church Castlecaulfield was installed in 1968 by the Apprentice Boys of Derry as a memorial to Revd Walker.

Reverend James Davidson

This clergyman was an important member of the United Irishmen in Tyrone. According to the records, this Presbyterian minister lived near Stewartstown. The United Irishmen had selected prospective members to serve for a proposed reformed parliament in Ireland, and Revd Davidson was to be one of the Tyrone members.

AN ABC SUMMARY OF TYRONE

A is for Altmore: home of General James Shields, a United States senator during the nineteenth century; **Ancestral Homes:** there are ancestral homes of three United States Presidents (Woodrow Wilson, James Buchanan and Ulysses Grant) in Tyrone, while removed and rebuilt at the Ulster American Folk Park is the ancestral home of Archbishop John Hughes of New York; **Ambrose the Pig:** a Strabane icon that celebrates the works of Brian O'Nolan.

B is for Border: Tyrone is bordered by no less than five other Ulster counties, hence the friendly rivalry when it comes to sporting events, such as the fiercely contested annual Ulster Gaelic Football Championship; **Bessy Bell Hill:** near Newtownstewart, it was named by Scottish settlers; **Battle of Benburb:** when Owen Roe O'Neill and his army defeated Munro's Scottish Army.

C is for Castlehill in Dungannon: where the ruins of a Tower House lie. During the tenth century this was the chief seat of the O'Neills of Tyrone; **Creggandevesky and Cregganconroe:** two megalithic tombs located close to each other in Mid-Tyrone; a special Tyrone **Cough Cure** that includes honey, flax seed and nutmeg.

D is for Devlin: one of the most popular Tyrone surnames; **Dooish Mountain** near **Drumquin; Derrylaughan and Derrytresk:** two adjacent communities in East Tyrone with Gaelic Athletic clubs.

E is for Eskragh Lough: near Dungannon; the theme of **Emigration** that has so often shaped the history of Tyrone and its people; the **Errigal Keerogue Cross** near the village of Ballygawley.

F is for Brian Friel: the internationally renowned playwright who produced such marvellous works as *Translations* and *Dancing at Lughnasa*; the **Fishing** around the Western shores of Lough Neagh that encompasses much of East Tyrone.

G is for Glenhull near Greencastle: an area where the last native speakers of Irish lived – and which was well documented by a research study by Michael J. Murphy in *Tyrone Folk Quest;* **Gortin Glen Forest Park,** a popular visitor attraction.

H is for Harry Avery's Castle in Newtownstewart: named after a fourteenth-century chieftain; **Mickey Harte:** highly successful Tyrone Gaelic football manager from the parish of Errigal Ciaran.

I is for Iggy Jones: from Dungannon, one of the finest players in the history of Gaelic football.

J is for jobs: created by local industries in the twentieth century such as Tyrone Brick and Tyrone Crystal.

K is for places such as Killeter in the west, **Killyclogher** in central Tyrone and **Kildress** in East Tyrone.

M is for the River Mourne which flows through Strabane; the **MacRory Cup** for Ulster Colleges: named in honour of Cardinal Joseph MacRory from Ballygawley.

N is for Newcomer: a popular term for the migrant workers who have enriched Tyrone life in recent years and helped to balance the trend between emigration and immigration; **Newmills:** a small but proud village community in South Tyrone.

O is for O'Neill: Tyrone is synonymous with this popular surname – and the trophy for the Club Senior Gaelic Football Championship in the county is appropriately named 'The O'Neill Cup'; Ogham was the written form of the Celtic Language – seen at Aghascrebagh.

P is for Portal Tomb: there are some in Tyrone, including the Ballyrenan Portal Tomb near Newtownstewart; the Mountains of Pomeroy: a popular ballad by Dr George Sigerson.

S is for Strule: the name of one of the rivers that runs through Omagh along with the Camowen and the Drumragh; Stangmore Park: where Dungannon Swifts, the soccer team who play in the Irish Premiership, are based.

T is for Turf: an energy source that has part-fuelled Tyrone over the centuries; *Townland Names of County Tyrone* and *Tyrone Folk Quest*: two important publications that have helped to preserve placename origins and customs in County Tyrone.

U is for Under the Bridge: two of Tyrone's main towns have large bridges; The Ulster American Folk Park at Camphill near Omagh is a magnificent visitor centre that explains how the Tyrone/Ulster/Irish emigrant survived in the 'new world'.

V is for Valley: the Clogher and Glenelly valleys are two fine examples.

W is for Washingbay: an area of healing according to tales of yesteryear; Willie Anderson: former captain of the Irish rugby team who bravely stood up to the New Zealand All Blacks' haka.

X marks the spot of where Hugh O'Neill departed Crieve Lough near Stewartstown in 1607 prior to the Flight of the Earls.

Y is for all the 'Yankee': links between Tyrone and America – such as poet John Montague, born in Brooklyn, New York but resident in the 'rough field' of Garvaghey.

Z is for Zarzecki and Zilionas: just two of the surnames of 'newcomer' families that are prevalent in Tyrone.

BIBLIOGRAPHY

BOOKS

Bardon, Jonathan, *A History of Ireland in 250 Episodes* (Gill & Macmillan Ltd, Dublin, 2008)

Bell, Robert, *The Book of Ulster Surnames* (The Blackstaff Press, Belfast, 1988)

Blair, May, *Hiring Fairs and Market Places* (Appletree Press, Belfast, 2007)

Boylan, Henry (ed.), *A Dictionary of Irish Biography* (Gill & Macmillan Ltd, 1999)

Byrne, Art and Sean McMahon, *Great Northerners* (Poolbeg Press, Dublin, 1991)

Carruthers, Mark and Stephen Douds (eds), *Stepping Stones: The Arts in Ulster 1971–2001* (The Blackstaff Press, Belfast, 2001)

Connolly, S. J. (ed.), *The Oxford Companion to Irish History* (Oxford University Press, 2007)

Department of the Environment for Northern Ireland, *Historic Monuments of Northern Ireland* (The Universities Press, Belfast, 1987)

Devlin, Polly, *The Far Side of the Lough: Stories from an Irish Childhood* (The O'Brien Press, Dublin, 1999 edition)

Dickson, R.J., *Ulster Emigration to Colonial America 1718–1785* (Routledge & Kegan Paul Ltd, London, 1966)

Dillon, Charles and Henry A. Jefferies (ed.), *Tyrone: History and Society* (Geography Publications, Dublin, 2000)

Donnelly, Daniel J., *The Sperrins and their Foothills* (R. & S. Printers, Monaghan, 2010)

Duncan, Tom et al., *The 1608 Royal Schools Celebrate 400 Years of History* (Premier Print, Armagh, 2008)

Fitzgerald, Patrick and Brian Lambkin, *Migration in Irish History, 1607–2007* (Palgrave Macmillan, 2008)

Flackes, W.D. and Sydney Elliott, *Northern Ireland: A Political Directory 1968–88* (The Blackstaff Press, Belfast, 1989)

Grimes, Pat: Memories of Lough Neagh, *The Heritage of the Fishing Families of Lough Neagh* (Ardboe Heritage, 2012)

Hamlin, Ann and Chris Lynn, *Pieces of the Past: Archaeological Excavations by the Department of the Environment for Northern Ireland 1970–1986* (HMSO, Belfast, 1988)

Harbison, Peter, *Guide to National and Historic Monuments of Ireland* (Gill & Macmillan, Dublin, 1992)

Hutchinson, W.R., *Tyrone Precinct: A History of the Plantation Settlement of Dungannon and Mountjoy to Modern Times* (W.E. Mayne, Belfast, 1951)

Killen, John, *The Irish Christmas Book* (The Blackstaff Press, Belfast, 1985)

Law, Gary, *The Cultural Traditions Dictionary* (The Blackstaff Press, Belfast, 1998)

Longley, Edna (ed.), *The Bloodaxe Book of 20th Century Poetry* (Bloodaxe Books, 2000)

Loughran, Michael et al., *Dungannon's Otherworld* ((Dungannon Development Association, 1989)

McAleer, Patrick, *Townland Names of County Tyrone: Their Meanings Explained* (Ashardan and Moyola Books, 1988 edition)

McCavitt, John, *The Flight of the Earls* (Gill & Macmillan Ltd, Dublin, 2005)

McEvoy, Brendan, *The United Irishmen in County Tyrone* (The Armagh Diocesan Historical Society, 1998)

McEvoy, John, *Statistical Survey of the County of Tyrone* (Graisberry and Campbell, Dublin, 1802)

McKay, Patrick and Kay Muhr, *Lough Neagh Places: Their Names and Origins* (Queen's University, Belfast, 2007)

McMahon, Sean, *A Short History of Ireland* (Mercier Press, Cork, 1996)

McRedmond, Louis, *Modern Irish Lives: A Dictionary of 20th Century Biography* (Gill & Macmillan Ltd, Dublin, 1998)

McVeigh, Frank, *Our Cornmill and Other Memories* (Dungannon Development Association, 1987)

Mallory, J.P. and T.E. McNeill, *The Archaeology of Ulster: From Colonization to Plantation* (Institute of Irish Studies, The Queen's University of Belfast, 1991)

Marshall, Ruth, *Celebrating Irish Festivals* (Hawthorn Press, 2003)

Marshall, W.F., *Livin' in Drumlister: The Collected Ballads and Verses of W.F. Marshall 'The Bard of Tyrone'* (The Blackstaff Press, Belfast, 1983)

Martin, Joe, *The GAA in Tyrone: The Long Road to Glory* (Tyrone County Board and Colour Books Limited, 2003 edition)

Miller, Kerby and Paul Wagner, *Out of Ireland: The Story of Irish Emigration to America* (Aurum Press, London, 1994)

Mitchell, Brian, *The Surnames of North West Ireland* (Clearfield Publishers, Baltimore, Maryland, 2010)

Murphy, Michael J., *Tyrone Folk Quest* (The Blackstaff Press, Belfast, 1973)

O'Donnell, Edward T., *1001 Things Everyone Should Know About Irish American History* (Broadway Books, New York, 2002)

O'Farrell, Padraic, *Irish Customs* (Gill & Macmillan Ltd, Dublin, 2004)

Rogers, Mary, *Prospect of Tyrone* (Watergate Press, Enniskillen, 1988)

Ryan D'Arcy, Mary, *The Saints of Ireland* (Mercier Press, Cork, 1985)

St Clair, Sheila, *Folklore of the Ulster People* (Mercier Press, Cork, 1971)

Vance, Rob, *Secrets of the Stones: Decoding Ireland's Lost Past* (2009)

Van Esbeck, Edmund, *Irish Rugby* (Ashfield Press, Dublin, 1999)

JOURNAL EXTRACTS

O'Conluain, Proinsias, *The Last Native Irish-Speakers of Tyrone: Dúiche Néill Journal of the O'Neill Country Historical Society*, No. 4 (1989)

WEBSITES

www.bbc.co.uk/ulsterscots/words

www.blessedpatrickoloughranprimaryschool.co.uk

www.carmengfc.com/nally-heritage-centre

www.castlecaulfield.wordpress.com

www.discoverni.com

www.discoverloughneagh.com

www.flavouroftyrone.com

www.multitext.ucc.ie

www.nationaltrust.org.uk

www.nidirect.gov.uk/forests-in-county-tyrone-2

www.nienvironmentlink.org/cmsfiles/files/Publications/Historic-Environment-1.pdf

www.ninis2.nisra.gov.uk

www.nisra.gov.uk

www.omaghbombmemorial.com

www.paulbrady.com

www.ulster-scots.com

www.ulsterhistory.co.uk

www.ulsterscotslanguage.com/en/texts/what-is-ulster-scots

www.workhouses.org.uk

GUIDES

Cookstown District Council
Dungannon District Council
Omagh District Council
Strabane District Council
The Life, Work and Legacy of W.F. Marshall: produced by the Ulster-Scots Community Network